VERS
Sept '06

Larry Verstraete

LOST TREASURES
True Stories of Discovery

Scholastic Canada Ltd.

Toronto New York London Auckland Sydney
Mexico City New Delhi Hong Kong Buenos Aires

For my nieces, nephews and their families
— treasures one and all

Scholastic Canada Ltd.
604 King Street West, Toronto, Ontario M5V 1E1, Canada

Scholastic Inc.
557 Broadway, New York, NY 10012, USA

Scholastic Australia Pty Limited
PO Box 579, Gosford, NSW 2250, Australia

Scholastic New Zealand Limited
Private Bag 94407, Greenmount, Auckland, New Zealand

Scholastic Children's Books
Euston House, 24 Eversholt Street, London NW1 1DB, UK

Library and Archives Canada Cataloguing in Publication

Verstraete, Larry
Lost treasures : true stories of discovery / Larry Verstraete.

ISBN 0-439-95739-7

1. Treasure troves—Juvenile literature. I. Title.

G525.V468 2006   j904   C2005-907559-7

6 5 4 3 2 1   Printed in Canada   06 07 08 09 10

Table of Contents

Acknowledgements

Many people have contributed to this book, and to each of them I owe a debt of gratitude. Thank you to . . .

- Haig Jacobs, Carlos Saavedra, Bill Seliger and the rest of the ROBCAR team for patiently guiding me through the story of the *Santa Maria de la Consolacion*
- Derek Erstelle for sharing his adventures and touring me through his personal collection of treasures
- the members of the Calgary Metal Detecting Club who welcomed me into their fold
- Anita Janzic of the Morden Museum, Alan Hildebrand of Prairie Meteorite Search and Daniel Gregorash of the Royal Tyrell Museum for their advice and expertise
- Vera Brandzin and Tara Baxter for information on the legalities of treasure seeking
- Barbara Hehner for carefully checking the facts, and Lori Burwash for insightful editing
- the Scholastic Canada team who worked so diligently to shape the book: Yüksel Hassan, Diane Kerner and especially Sandra Bogart Johnston, Senior Editor, who so ably guided the project, offered suggestions and provided much appreciated encouragement
- fellow members of Writers' Group — Faith Anderson, Judy Pirnie, Lisa Sykes, and Janet Tomy — for their wise words
- Stephen and Ashley, my children, who listened and coached from the sidelines
- my wife, Jo, who believed in the project and accompanied me on treasure-seeking ventures along the way

Introduction

Kip Wagner spotted it while walking along a shell-strewn Florida beach. Sue Hendrickson's looked like an ordinary chunk of rock. Ten-year-old Bingham Bryant's was gathering dust in his school library.

Treasure means different things to different people. It comes in many forms and shapes, and is just waiting to be discovered. What is considered valuable, rare or of great worth varies from one person to the next.

For Kip Wagner a few silver coins washed up along the beach led to the discovery of a fleet of sunken Spanish galleons — and a treasure worth millions.

Sue Hendrickson's strange rock was actually a fossil vertebra, part of a huge *T. Rex* skeleton, the largest ever found. Today Sue, the dinosaur, stands on display in the Field Museum in Chicago where Sue, the paleontologist, can visit the skeleton that was named after her in recognition of her find.

Bingham Bryant discovered a long-lost masterpiece that had been sitting on a bookcase in his school for decades, unnoticed and unappreciated. It sold at auction for more than $600,000.

Have *you* ever dreamed of finding treasure? Have you imagined yourself stumbling across something rare or valuable that has been abandoned, forgotten, misplaced or overlooked by others? From pirate booty and exotic coins to rare fossils and lost artworks, the lure of treasure is irresistible.

In this book, you will read about great treasure hunts, follow treasure hunters on their quests, discover where their treasures are on display, and learn some treasure-hunting secrets along the way. So get ready for adventure.

And on the way, look for this icon:
It will tell you where the treasure is located, or the museum where it now resides.

Many Kinds of Treasure

Treasure has many meanings and takes many forms — from ancient coins to rare stamps to pirate gold. Here are some treasure terms you'll find in the book:

antiquity: an object dating from ancient times

artifact: an object made by a human being

booty: seized or stolen valuables; plunder

cache: a hidden store of things, usually weapons or valuables

collectible: an object that is collected for pleasure or profit, such as a stamp or coin

gem: a precious stone

hoard: a pile of hidden valuables

masterpiece: an exceptional creative work, such as a film, sculpture or painting

mint condition: description for a used object that is in new or perfect condition

motherlode: a vein or streak of gold or other precious metal in the earth's crust

nugget: a lump of gold or other precious metal in its natural state

piece of eight: a silver coin used in Spain and its colonies between 1500 and 1800

trove: valuable items that have been deliberately hidden by someone who intended to recover them later

Chapter 1
PIRATE TREASURE

In Their Own Words

"I realized that Bellamy's bones could literally be under my fingers. With every thrust into the sand, I reached for the lid to a coffin."
Barry Clifford, describing his chilling search for the Whydah, *a sunken pirate ship*

"It doesn't matter what others believe. I'm convinced, and that's enough for me to carry on."
Dan Blankenship, determined Oak Island treasure hunter

"Bill found the first coin on the site. He became so excited that he screamed and spat out his regulator."
Diver Haig Jacobs on finding the wreck of the Santa Maria de la Consolacion *and her treasure*

"The path that must be followed to find my treasure," Captain Kidd, 1691
Message on a map found hidden in a wooden chest belonging to Hubert Palmer

Chapter 1 ~ **PIRATE TREASURE**

Expedition Whydah *Sea Lab & Learning Center,*
Provincetown, Massachusetts

The Search for
Black Sam's Treasure

All his life Barry Clifford had heard stories of Sam Bellamy and his ship, the Whydah. *He dreamed of finding the pirate's lost ship and its vast treasure. He dreamed of solving a mystery 250 years in the making.*

April 26, 1717

Black Sam Bellamy, the pirate captain, scoured the Atlantic Ocean with a watchful eye. A monster storm was brewing. All the signs were there. Dark clouds swirling along the horizon. White-crested waves pounding the hull, spewing water over the deck. Gusts of wind attacking the sails. The ship's masts groaning and creaking under the pressure. The storm was almost upon them.

> **Men and treasure poured into the swirling ocean. The broken ship disappeared, swallowed completely by sand and sea.**

Bellamy knew he and his crew had to steer clear of the shoreline, with its hidden sandbars and shallow beaches. He ordered his ship, the *Whydah*, into deeper waters and signalled the four other ships in his fleet to do the same.

The *Whydah* was Bellamy's pride. Sleek and sturdy, capable of great speed, it made an ideal pirate ship. For months, Bellamy and his fleet had sailed the ocean, outrunning other vessels, capturing them, plundering their treasures. Now, heavy with gold and silver from at least 53 vessels, the ships were heading north, returning home to Cape Cod, a spit of land near Boston, Massachusetts. It was time to divide the treasure, repair the ships and plan the next move.

Sam Bellamy had another reason to get to Cape Cod — Maria Hallett.

Maria was the love of Bellamy's life. They made a fine match. He in his twenties, ruggedly handsome, wild and carefree. She only sixteen, a beauty with flowing hair and sparkling blue eyes.

Bellamy knew that Maria was waiting for him.

But the storm came sooner than expected, and Bellamy could not escape it fast enough. Tossed by wild winds, pounded by waves three storeys high, the *Whydah* was pushed to shore, thrust against a sandbar stern first and smashed by a wall of water. Its sails and masts collapsed, and the ship rolled on its side. Cannons snapped from their mounts, knocked out support beams and plunged through the deck, crushing sailors and pinning them to the wreck.

A mountainous wave pulverized the hull, splitting it in two, cracking it wide open. Men and treasure poured into the swirling ocean. The broken ship disappeared, swallowed completely by sand and sea.

The crew never had a chance. Most drowned. A few hung on, only to be crushed when the ship rolled on its side. Of the 146 pirates aboard, just 2 survived.

For days after the storm, bodies littered the beach, washed ashore along with broken timber and lost cargo. Broken-hearted Maria Hallett walked the coastline, examining each bloated body, checking to see if any was her beloved Sam.

She never found him. Black Sam Bellamy was dead, swept away and lost to the sea.

~

More than 250 years later . . .

From the time he was a young boy growing up in Mas-

sachusetts, Barry Clifford was fascinated by tales of the *Whydah*. The ship had disappeared almost in his backyard. According to Thomas Davis, one of the surviving pirates, its cargo included 180 bags of gold and silver stored in chests below deck. By some accounts, the treasure was worth millions.

To Clifford, a diver, the *Whydah*'s story was tragic and sad, but also full of exciting possibilities. He dreamed of finding the lost ship.

Many warned Clifford that it was useless to even try. The region where the wreck occurred was treacherous, they said. A graveyard of lost ships. The water was cold, deep and criss-crossed by wild currents. The sands were shifting, thin as soup in places. Objects trapped on the ocean bottom often disappeared without a trace.

Besides, people liked to add, hadn't others already tried to find the *Whydah* and failed? People like Cyprian Southack, a map-maker and sea captain who had arrived on the scene barely a week after the *Whydah* tragedy. Sent by the governor of Massachusetts, he was charged with salvaging the wreck and its booty. Looters had already picked through the remains, plucking what they could from the sea. Southack did his own search, carefully combing the shoreline, questioning local residents for leads to the missing treasure. After nine days of trying, he gave up. There was little left to find. Southack gathered his charts and maps, packed his bags and scurried home.

Barry Clifford knew of Southack and his failed venture. He also knew of a map drawn by Southack that showed the coastline at the time of the disaster. On the map, near the town of Billingsgate, Southack had written: "The treasure ship *Whido* lost." The map gave Clifford hope. He was sure the *Whido*, or *Whydah*, was still out there.

Clifford compared Southack's drawings to modern aerial photographs of the area. Wind and water had eroded the coast-

line since the tragedy. Billingsgate no longer existed. The wreck of the *Whydah*, if it had survived at all, was likely no longer in the spot Southack had indicated.

> *The map gave Clifford hope. He was sure the* Whido*, or* Whydah*, was still out there.*

Clifford reread Southack's letters and journals, noting names of towns and places; carefully, he charted these points with coloured pins on a large wall map. The cluster of pins was a start, the beginning of a search pattern. To find the *Whydah*, though, Clifford needed to explore below the waterline.

In 1982 he obtained a permit from the Massachusetts Board of Underwater Archaeological Resources. He chartered a boat and, with the help of friends, headed out to sea towing a magnetometer over the area suggested by the pins on the map. The magnetometer, an instrument that detects magnetic shifts from iron beneath the water, would help to locate anchors, bells, cannons and other traces of the doomed ship.

Using the magnetometer readings, Clifford created a more detailed map of the search area. There were hundreds of points, a multitude of possible locations. Were any of these the *Whydah?* There was only one way to find out — send divers below to investigate. That, Clifford knew, would take a lot of time and money.

In 1983 Clifford pitched his idea to a number of businessmen. He told the story of Black Sam and Maria Hallett, of the lost ship and the immense treasure that lay below the sea. Would you like to be part of history? he asked. Part of the team that finds the *Whydah* and her riches? In a short time, Clifford had a group of investors to back his search.

With the investors' money, he bought a research vessel and equipped it with the latest diving equipment. Then he hired a

Chapter 1 ~ **PIRATE TREASURE**

crew and, armed with his maps, set out to sea to investigate the strongest hits pinpointed by the magnetometer.

The task was daunting. The dive season was short, only a few months long, and the sea was often unruly. Waves rocked the boat, twisting lines and churning the stomachs of the crew onboard. There were hundreds of sites to investigate, and by the end of the summer only a handful had been searched. Money was dwindling quickly and frustration was high.

> Once a diver came to the surface holding something cylindrical and heavy — a bomb. The site, they soon realized, was a dump site for discarded weapons and ammunition from soldiers practising manoeuvres and anti-aircraft drills during World War II.

During the winter Clifford reviewed his research, looking for hidden clues and missed opportunities. The next year the search continued, again with little success. The crew located other wrecks, but not the *Whydah*. The investors were growing restless, and Clifford fought to keep their spirits alive. The *Whydah* was out there, lurking in the sand, he argued. Sam Bellamy had walked upon its decks, ordered its immense sails unfurled, led its crew to attack, and now the pirate ship and its great treasure was calling to them, waiting to be found.

In the spring of 1984, the crew resumed the search. Clifford felt that, in a strange way, Sam Bellamy was with them, guiding the hunt. Bellamy's body had never been found, his fate never determined. Yet Clifford often dreamed of the pirate captain and felt his presence at every turn.

Each night Clifford reread Southack's journal and studied his maps, hoping to uncover new information. "I realized that Bellamy's bones could literally be under my fingers," Clifford wrote in his book *Expedition Whydah*. "With every thrust into the sand, I reached for the lid to a coffin."

On the afternoon of July 19, the crew headed to a spot about 460 metres from shore, a site that had been mapped earlier. The readings weren't the strongest there, but they had been consistent and frequent. It was getting late in the day, and a storm was brewing. Dark clouds swirled along the horizon. Thunder rumbled across the sky. Clifford shivered. He remembered the story of the day the *Whydah* went down. It must have been like this, he thought.

Divers searched the ocean floor. Within ten minutes, they surfaced. "We've found something . . . a big piece of iron," they reported.

Lightning flashed. The sky was growing darker.

One diver went back under and resurfaced in minutes, his face breaking into a huge grin. "A cannon!" he shouted.

Within seconds the sea was awash with divers, all of them

A diver searches the ocean floor for wreckage from the *Whydah*.

anxious to see the find for themselves. Clifford jumped in, too. About 6 metres below the surface, he spotted three heavily encrusted cannon muzzles poking through the sand. Then he found other objects, some round, the size of baseballs, others oblong and larger. All of them were covered with centuries of heavy sediment and residue. Clifford pried a grapefruit-sized object loose and hauled it to the surface. Using his knife, he picked away at the crust.

As streaks of lightning blazed across the sky and drops of rain pelted the boat, Clifford realized what he was holding. "A cannonball," he said.

But there was something else, too. A flat object, small and round. Clifford rubbed the sand away. It was a blackened silver coin. A date was stamped on it: *1684*.

The sky was black now, the rain coming down in heavy sheets. To Clifford it was as if Sam Bellamy were there, speaking to them, congratulating them on their find.

That night Clifford couldn't sleep. "I stared at the ceiling," he wrote, "half expecting Samuel Bellamy to appear like a genie from a bottle and give me a salute."

> **Beside a cannon they found a leg bone.**

For the rest of that season and all of the next, the team dived again and again, hauling up hundreds of gold and silver coins. They also recovered gold bars, pistols, pewter plates, dishes and navigational equipment. Each artifact was carefully catalogued, cleaned and preserved.

Some finds were more chilling than others. Beside a cannon they found a leg bone along with a leather shoe and a white stocking. It was an eerie reminder of the past, of the ship's terrible end and the fate of the people who had once walked upon its decks.

The site was rich in treasure, and it was obvious that Clifford and his crew had made a significant find. But was this

really the *Whydah*, or was it some other warship? More proof was needed.

In September 1985 they got it. Lying on its side, half buried in sand near a cannon, they found a ship's bell. When the crust was loosened and peeled away, they discovered evidence no one could deny. The bell was engraved *The Whydah Gally 1716*.

This was Sam Bellamy's ship, and this was his plundered treasure.

The *Whydah*'s treasure has been valued at over $400 million. Although more than one hundred thousand artifacts have been recovered, divers still explore the site. Rather than sell the artifacts they discovered, Clifford and his investors opened a museum. At the Expedition *Whydah* Sea Lab & Learning Center in Provincetown, Massachusetts, visitors can see the *Whydah* bell, coins, bones retrieved from the wreck and weapons such as cannons, cannonballs and muskets. For Barry Clifford, the thrill of the hunt continues. He has been involved in searches for

Barry Clifford with pieces of eight salvaged from the *Whydah*.

other sunken ships, but the *Whydah* holds a special place for him. "Even though I have searched for sunken ships all over the world, I am always drawn back to the *Whydah*. I continue to search for everything that will tell me the whole story."

Perhaps Clifford is not alone in his search. Locals claim that on windswept nights, when the waves crash upon the Cape, they can sometimes hear the ghost of Maria Hallett wailing above the din as she combs the shore looking for her lost love, Black Sam Bellamy.

Treasure Tips

Tales of treasure are everywhere. Perhaps even in your own neighbourhood!

Some stories of lost treasure go back only a generation or two. The memory of the event may still be fresh in the minds of people who lived at the time. With a few well-placed questions, some patience and an eagerness to listen, it might be possible for you to unravel the tale.

Tom Michalski, an American diver and dive shop owner, is a treasure hunter who knows how to dig into the past. For thirty years, Michalski has researched tales of lost treasure around Lake Coeur d'Alene, Idaho. By carefully listening to people's stories, he has been able to track down and recover heaps of treasure at the bottom of the lake, including, among other things, sixteen shipwrecks, five cars and mounds of antique bottles, dishes, guns, watches and wedding rings.

Digging the Money Pit

A weather-beaten block and tackle dangled from the oak tree. Below it, the ground formed a strange saucer-shaped depression. Pirate treasure, for sure, Daniel McGinnis figured.

One warm morning in April 1795, sixteen-year-old Daniel McGinnis rowed across Mahone Bay. He had his sights set on Oak Island, a rocky island off the coast of Nova Scotia.

McGinnis had heard stories about Oak Island. Some people believed it was once home to pirates and buried treasure. Others claimed it was haunted. Strange lights of unexplained origin had been spotted there. Spook lights, locals called them.

McGinnis had come to check out the tales, perhaps even fetch a souvenir to prove his bravery. A gold coin or two would be nice. Even better would be a pistol, knife or other pirate weapon.

After spending the morning exploring the island, McGinnis ended up empty-handed and discouraged, but in the early after-noon he stumbled upon a small clearing. Beneath a gnarled oak tree, he found a saucer-shaped depression in the ground. A ship's block and tackle dangled from a sawed-off branch about 5 metres above the ground. The limb was scarred and worn. It looked as if someone had dug a pit beneath the tree and, using the branch as a support, lowered something into the ground.

Pirate treasure? McGinnis wasn't sure, but he meant to find out. The next day he returned with two friends, twenty-year-old John Smith and thirteen-year-old Anthony Vaughan. They car-ried picks and shovels and were excited by the prospect of find-ing pirate treasure. They'd have the pit dug out in no time.

Dirt flew. With three of them working, it didn't take long to dig a hole more than a metre deep. Then their shovels clanked against something hard — flagstones set in a circle. The ground

Chapter 1 ~ **PIRATE TREASURE**

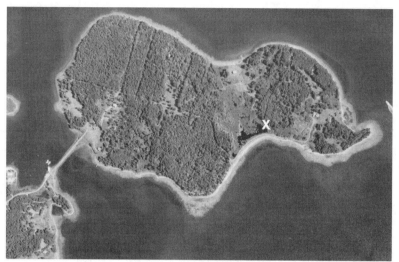

An aerial photograph of Oak Island showing the location of the Money Pit.

around the flagstones looked strangely different. Hard-packed, for one thing. Chipped and chiselled, for another. It looked as if someone had tried to dig around the stones before.

The boys pried the flagstones loose and set them aside. They were on to something now. They dug faster, eager to find the treasure that certainly lay below. Two metres farther, their tools struck something hollow-sounding. A wooden chest? Hopes soared.

The boys tore at the dirt, exposing a platform of oak logs wedged into the sides of the pit, and freed the logs from the tightly packed dirt. Underneath there was only more rock-hard clay — and with that came disappointment.

The digging grew more difficult. The ground was firm — like cement — and by now the pit was far deeper than the boys were tall. Hauling out the dirt was back-breaking work. Progress was slow and nightfall was fast approaching. The boys gave up for the day, tired but determined. Someone had gone through a lot of trouble to build the pit, and that meant only one thing. Something valuable was below.

Every day for weeks, the boys rowed to the island to dig. They rigged a new block and tackle to the old scarred limb to hoist out the soil. Slowly the shaft grew deeper. At the 6-metre level, they hit a second platform and, at 9 metres, a third.

The hole was massive now, 4 metres across and several storeys deep. Realizing they could go no farther on their own, the boys told their parents and neighbours of the find. Imagine the riches below, they said. Pirate treasure, for sure. But no one was interested. The island was haunted, the boys were told, possessed by ghosts, a place to avoid. Unable to continue by themselves, the boys abandoned the dig.

Eight years passed. The boys became men. Both McGinnis and Smith married and built homes on Oak Island, but the dream of treasure stayed with all three. They yearned for the day when they could dig again.

In 1803 the men found a group of people who would provide money and equipment to continue. The Onslow Company was established, and digging resumed. At 12 metres, diggers struck a fourth platform of logs. There was a fifth at 15 metres, and still others every 3 metres. Just below the platform at the 18-metre level, excavators found a thick layer of coconut fibre. Coconuts didn't grow on the island, only in southern climates thousands of kilometres away. Places visited by pirates, perhaps? The lure of treasure grew even stronger.

> *In 1849 the stone was reportedly decoded as saying, "Forty feet below, two million pounds are buried."*

Beneath the log platform at the 27-metre level, the workmen discovered a thin, dark green, rectangular stone almost a metre long with hieroglyphics etched into one side. They removed the stone and examined it carefully. What was the message — a warning, a clue? The

stone was of a material unknown to Nova Scotia. The letters were foreign and indecipherable. In 1849 the stone was reportedly decoded as saying, "Forty feet below, two million pounds are buried."

Excitement gripped the crew. They had to be almost on top of the treasure now. Digging continued. Then, on a Saturday evening, with the hole 30 metres deep, a rod was pounded through the clay to probe below. It struck something wooden and hollow. A hidden vault. But the sun was setting and the next day was Sunday, a day of rest. The crew put their shovels aside, vowing to return at first light on Monday.

Disappointment greeted the men Monday morning. Water had seeped into the pit and filled the hole. They tried pumping out the water, but the hole filled again. Then they tried sinking a second shaft alongside the first, determined to tunnel across to the bottom of the old one. But the new shaft was too close to the first, its walls too thin to support the pressure of rock and water. The shaft collapsed, water swamped the new pit, and three men drowned in the swirling chaos. Discouraged and out of money, the men abandoned the project. If there was treasure in the Money Pit, as the shaft was dubbed, it was impossible to reach.

But the dream is irresistible. It refuses to die. In the two hundred years since the first attempt, more than half a dozen groups have tried to find treasure on Oak Island. New shafts have been dug, more holes drilled, other tunnels added. Heavy equipment has been called into duty — cranes, hydraulics, super-sized pumps. The latest scientific devices and methods have been put to use — sonar, X-rays, carbon dating. The island has been poked, prodded, probed and investigated. Millions of dollars have been spent, and six lives have been lost.

Each attempt has met with failure. There seems to be a network of tunnels that flood the shafts with water. The tunnels

Pumping water out of the pit. Despite a number of well-organized attempts, the route to the Money Pit continues to elude treasure seekers.

may connect to the ocean, the water in them rising and falling with the tides.

Along the way there have been interesting twists in the Oak Island puzzle. In 1849 treasure seekers pulled three small links of gold chain out of a shaft, the first evidence of possible wealth below. In 1897 a tiny piece of parchment was found. In 1976

Chapter 1 ~ **PIRATE TREASURE**

treasure hunters lowered an underwater camera into the flooded shaft. Watery images of oak chests and a severed hand fluttered across the screen.

Questions abound. Is there really treasure on Oak Island? Whose treasure? How did it get there? Some believe the notorious pirate Captain Kidd hid his vast fortune on the island. Others argue that the British army, retreating from the Americans in the Revolutionary War, landed on Oak Island and built the pit to hide their war chests and payroll. Still others speculate that an immense royal treasure lies in the pit, gold and jewels deposited for safekeeping by a king or queen in a time of revolution.

Excavation of Oak Island continues. New treasure hunters — the lure of riches deep in their veins — have taken up the quest, hopeful that one day they might crack the mystery of Oak Island and uncover the treasure it holds.

Dan Blankenship is one of them. As the island's longest-serving treasure hunter, he has spent decades probing Oak Island. He has sunk his own personal fortune into the project and narrowly escaped death when a shaft collapsed around him. Still he refuses to give up — faith and trust drive him. "It doesn't matter what others believe," Blankenship says. "I'm convinced, and that's enough for me to carry on."

Treasure Under Construction

Generating Treasure

In 2004, when workers from Nova Scotia Power lowered the levels of the Mersey River in order to make repairs to 70-year-old generating stations, they found more than mud and rocks beneath the water. Hundreds of artifacts appeared along the exposed riverbed. Pottery, spear points, knives, axes, barbed harpoons and a multitude of other items — some of them eight thousand years old — were found around 109 ancient camp-sites along the river.

To archeologists, the discovery is a bounty of riches. The artifacts are evidence that long before Europeans came to North America, a thriving civilization — the Mi'kmaq people — occupied the region. By collecting and studying the arti-facts, archeologists hope to learn more about the Mi'kmaq and a little-known period of Canada's history.

To descendents of the Mi'kmaq, the discovery is an oppor-tunity to touch the past in a very personal way. Says Roger Lewis, a Mi'kmaq archaeologist working on the site: "It was a humbling experience, discovering just how organized and knowledgeable our ancestors were."

 Mammoth Site, Hot Springs, South Dakota

Death Trap

In June 1974 George Hanson, a bulldozer operator, hit something unexpectedly hard at a construction site in Hot Springs, South Dakota. When he stopped his machine and climbed down for a closer look, he saw a 2-metre-long tusk and other bones in the red dirt. They turned out to be mammoth bones, the remains of giant elephant-like prehistoric animals. Excavations of the site revealed other wonders beneath the dirt. Besides the skeletons of more than 50 mammoths, paleontologists found the fossil bones of extinct camels, bears and other animals. Some twenty-six thousand years ago, they believe, the site was a giant sinkhole, a watery death trap for thousands of prehistoric creatures.

 The British Museum, London, England

Shiny Things

In 1979, after spending an unsuccessful afternoon prospecting with a metal detector, Arthur and Gretha Brooks drove to a freshly bulldozed construction site in Thetford, England, for one last try. The sun was setting, and they were heading back to the car after another frustrating attempt when the metal detector gave off a sharp signal. Arthur stooped to clear away the dirt while Gretha looked on.

"I stood above him," she said later, "and suddenly we saw a shiny thing, and a little black box, and as we pulled them out we saw there were other things round them in wet sand. There

were spikes sticking up." The spikes turned out to be the handles of spoons buried vertically in the dirt. Around the spoons, the pair found other items — necklaces, beads, bracelets, rings and pendants. The spoons bore the name of Faunus, a god worshipped by pagan farmers and shepherds. Because the treasure was found near a well-known ancient ceremonial site, archaeologists believe it may have been buried as a ritual offering during a period of Roman occupation in the fourth century. Experts estimated the Thetford Treasure to be worth £262,000 at the time of its discovery.

 Israel Museum, Jerusalem, Israel

Tomb Crusher

When a dump truck accidentally smashed through the roof of a tomb in the Jerusalem Peace Forest in November 1990, an ossuary (a stone burial box containing bones) was found inside. The ossuary was decorated with fine carvings and had a name engraved along the side: *Yehosef bar Qafa* (Joseph son of Caiaphas). The ossuary contained the bones of six people, all from one family: two infants, a child aged two to five, a boy aged thirteen to eighteen, a woman, and a man about sixty years old. The bones of the man are believed to be those of Caiaphas, the High Priest who questioned Jesus before his death.

Lost Treasure Off Dead Man's Island

Something in the fisherman's catch caught his attention. It was a clue to great treasure and a reminder of death and violence long ago.

1681

The Spanish galleon was the perfect pirate target. Alone. Bloated with treasure. Sluggish and slow. The *Santa Maria de la Consolacion* was ripe for the taking, and Bartholomew Sharpe, a cutthroat English pirate, meant to have her.

Of all the dangers on the ocean, pirates were among the most feared, and Bartholomew Sharpe was one of the worst. He had a reputation for being ruthless, cruel and unrelenting. Already he'd captured one Spanish ship after another, stripping them of treasure and murdering those who stood in his way.

And now he had his sights on the *Santa Maria de la Consolacion*.

The *Consolacion* carried a fortune, a hull crammed with silver coins, gold ingots and silver bars — treasure bound for the king's coffers in Spain. The cargo weighed the ship down, making it slow and difficult to manoeuvre. And the ship sailed alone. Normally Spanish ships travelled together, a handful of ships in a protective fleet. Somehow the *Consolacion* had become separated from the others. Sharpe ordered his six ships to give chase.

But Sharpe hadn't counted on Juan de Lerma, the captain of the *Consolacion*. De Lerma was a cunning, determined man, fiercely loyal to Spain. He would not give up his ship without a fight. When he spotted the six pirate ships bearing down on him, he flew into action. The pirate ships were sleeker, lighter and gaining steadily. Like bloodhounds giving chase, they were closing in for the kill. De Lerma knew he couldn't outrun them, but perhaps he could outsmart them.

De Lerma remembered Santa Clara Island, a tiny hump of rock about 50 kilometres off the coast of Ecuador. It wasn't too far away — maybe he could reach the island ahead of the pirates, find shelter in one of its coves, even set up a base to defend the ship from attack. He ordered ropes unleashed, rigging secured and sails unfurled. Men scrambled across the deck, eager to obey, anxious to escape. The *Consolacion* picked up speed.

But as the vessel neared the island, it scraped to an unexpected halt. In the rush, the crew hadn't noticed a reef hidden a few metres below the waterline. The collision ruptured the ship's hull, and as the *Consolacion* limped onward, its cargo tumbled into the sea.

> *Sharpe gave a final command: "Execute them all."*

De Lerma gave the order to flee. Small boats were lowered. Passengers and crew scrambled aboard and rowed to the nearby island.

The pirates were not far off, de Lerma realized. They would find the ship and her treasure and reap the rewards. Determined not to let that happen, he ordered the vessel torched, sending the ship's charred remains and its treasure to the ocean bottom.

By the time Sharpe arrived at the scene, nothing was left of the *Consolacion*. Angry at the loss of the treasure, he ordered his crew to round up the Spanish captain and his passengers. Then he gave a final command: "Execute them all."

After beheading the prisoners, an estimated 350 people, Sharpe stayed on the island for a few days. His crew forced several native fishermen to try to recover the treasure, but strong currents and dangerous sharks hampered the search. All they managed to salvage were a few sails and some rigging. Sharpe left the island, discouraged but not beaten. There were other ships on the ocean, other treasures ready for the picking.

Chapter 1 ~ **PIRATE TREASURE**

The locals, though, remembered Sharpe's bloody deeds. They nicknamed the island El Muerto, or Dead Man's Island. The name stuck, but the reasons behind it soon became lost in the swirl of history, just as the *Consolacion* became a distant memory deep below the treacherous waters.

~

In the 1980s a fisherman hauled an unusual object from the waters just north of Santa Clara Island. It was gnarled, caked with encrustations and hardly the catch he was expecting that day. But it was a prize nevertheless and, as it turned out, one more valuable than any fish he could have pulled from the sea. The object was an old ship anchor. Blackened by time, misshapen by sea growth, it had been in the water for centuries.

> **Blackened by time, misshapen by sea growth, the anchor had been in the water for centuries.**

News of the fisherman's catch reached Roberto Aguiire, the wealthy Ecuadorian owner of the fishing fleet. All his life, Aguiire had been fascinated by tales of lost treasure and dreamed of embarking on a treasure hunt of his own. Was there a shipwreck lurking below the waters near Santa Clara Island? he wondered.

For ten years, Aguiire let the question simmer while he slowly gathered information about the find. The anchor's shape and construction were clues to its past. Experts identified it as belonging to a seventeenth-century Spanish galleon.

In the 1990s, convinced that a full-fledged search was in order, Aguiire established ROBCAR, a salvage company. He appointed Carlos Saavedra as project manager, secured permits from the government of Ecuador to conduct a search, and hired divers to scour the ocean near the site where the anchor had been found.

A salvage ship near El Muerto, Dead Man's Island.

The divers found pottery, copper pots and other artifacts. The most amazing discovery, though, was a trail of Spanish coins, thousands of them, black and swollen with sea growth, strewn all over the ocean floor. All the coins were dated between 1650 and 1680.

Aguiire hired Robert Marx, a noted archaeologist and historian, to dig through mountains of Spanish records. The Spanish had kept detailed records of the ships in their fleet, listing the name of each vessel, its cargo, the dates it had sailed and the routes it had followed. Many Spanish ships, it turned out, had sailed from Peru to Panama, carrying gold and silver destined for Spain. Had one disappeared near Santa Clara Island?

The process was monotonous, requiring many hours of dogged work, but eventually Marx's efforts were rewarded. On an old seafaring map, he found this single line: "At this Island in this year of 1681 was cast away a rich ship."

The island was Santa Clara.

Chapter 1 ~ PIRATE TREASURE

A passage in another document produced a second clue. "In the year 1681 Captain Sharpe gave chase to a ship in this sea and the[r]e was lost on fowle ground near S. Clara in her 100,000 pieces of eight besides Plate and other goods of value."

Hopes soared. The story of Sharpe's chase, de Lerma's defeat and the fate of the *Consolacion* and her passengers had been documented by both the British and Spanish. Could the coins and artifacts found off the island have come from this particular ship?

Believing the treasure belonged to the *Consolacion,* Aguiire poured more money into a full-scale search. Magnetometer readings were taken to pinpoint the most likely search sites. Then divers scoured the ocean, pulling seven thousand coins out of the water in a matter of months. They also found pottery, small bronze signal cannons, pieces of large copper cooking

> *Once again hopes rose, then just as quickly faded.*

pots, cases of iron spikes and nails — even a crate of iron shoes for mules. The coin trail was wide. Starting a kilometre away from the island, it ran north to south in an almost straight line. The dates on the coins (none dated later than 1680, the year before the *Consolacion* sank), the wide sweep of the debris trail and the types of artifacts found in the water were consistent with the story of the doomed ship. But where was the shipwreck itself?

In 2001 another fisherman snagged his net on something in the waters off Dead Man's Island. Rather than lose the net, he asked ROBCAR divers to help him remove it. The snag was over a kilometre away from the coin trail, well outside the search area. To the divers' surprise, the net was caught on large ship timbers. Tests on the wood indicated that the timbers were centuries old. Was this the *Consolacion?*

Once again hopes rose, then just as quickly faded. There

was no other evidence of the *Consolacion* in the area, and the ROBCAR team was forced to conclude that the wreck was not the Spanish galleon after all, but a later wreck, possibly a whaling ship from the 1800s.

The search continued. For the next few seasons, divers followed the main trail, finding more coins and artifacts, but still no sign of the shipwreck itself.

In October 2004, led by magnetometer readings taken years earlier, ROBCAR diver and cameraman Haig Jacobs searched a region northeast of the coin trail. There he discovered a beautiful, intact olive jar outside of the main search area.

Believing they were on to something, the dive team returned a few months later. On January 21, 2005, during a sweep of the region, Bill Seliger, ROBCAR's magnetometer specialist, obtained a particularly strong reading. The next day, when

Haig Jacobs holds a *vasiga*, or olive jar.

Spanish *reals* from the *Consolacion* atop a map of Santa Clara Island.

Jacobs and Seliger dove to the site, they found large masses of encrusted formations rising slightly above the sea floor.

"Our hand-held magnetometer sang like a canary, indicating a large mass of iron metal below the surface," Haig reported. "Bill hand-fanned slightly and discovered three pieces of pottery, fused to the conglomerate. Clearly, they had been there for many years to have become encrusted in such a way."

> **There was no doubt — this was the Consolacion.**

The following day the crew returned with a small boat that had a blower attached. Using the blower, they swept aside sediment, revealing objects hidden for centuries on the ocean floor.

"Bill found the first coin on the site," Jacobs said. "He became so excited that he screamed and spat out his regulator."

This was the proof they needed — coins dated 1680, large masses of ceramics fused together by time, mounds on the ocean floor hiding evidence sunk long ago, a trail of debris pointing the way to the site. There was no doubt — this was the *Consolacion* and her priceless treasure, the prize that had slipped from Bartholomew Sharpe's grasp centuries before.

Divers continue their work at the site, prying treasure from the sea and putting the puzzling pieces of a long-forgotten story together again.

Treasure Tips

When it comes to tales of treasure, it is often difficult to separate truth from fiction. To get at the facts, treasure hunters rely on original records. First-hand historical accounts like those in diaries, journals, government documents, church registers, maps, newspaper reports and books written during the period in question are likely to be more factual and accurate than second-hand stories or sources. The more often a detail is repeated in original records, the more likely it is to be true and reliable.

Missing Maps, Lost Treasure

Hidden in the pirate's desk, his sea chest and other pieces of furniture, Hubert Palmer found old maps. He was certain they held the secret to Captain Kidd's long lost treasure, if only he could decipher the clues.

Somewhere, possibly in your basement or attic, perhaps tucked in an old trunk or dresser drawer, maps may be hiding — old, likely tattered at the edges, crinkled and brittle. Hardly special-looking. Barely worth a second glance.

And that may be why the maps have seldom been found. Their ordinariness is deceiving. It's difficult to imagine that the maps are valuable. It's difficult to believe they may lead to something greater — a treasure hidden centuries ago.

~

Hubert Palmer, a British lawyer, was considered by many to be an expert on pirates. He had a massive collection of pirate objects. Old manuscripts, yellowed and crisp. Sails, tattered and soiled. Black flags stamped with skulls and crossbones. Rusty pistols, long daggers — weapons of all kinds.

But a particular desk that Palmer had purchased from an antique dealer in 1929 was the pride of his collection. The desk was large and heavy, constructed of solid oak, its surface scratched and worn from long use. It had numerous drawers and compartments, some of them cleverly fashioned and practically invisible. Inside the desk was fastened a tarnished brass plate engraved with the words:

Captain William Kidd
Adventure Galley – 1669

Palmer was convinced that the desk in his study once belonged to William Kidd, the notorious pirate captain. It certainly looked like it was made in the seventeenth century, and the words and date on the brass plate matched Kidd's story perfectly.

In the late 1600s Kidd had prowled the oceans aboard his ship, *Adventure Galley*. He attacked merchant vessels with vengeance, seized their cargoes and amassed a fortune in jewels, precious stones, costly silks and other goods. Eventually, however, justice prevailed. Kidd was captured and convicted of murder and piracy. In 1701 he was taken to the gallows in London, England, and hanged. The rope broke on the first try, and Kidd was forced back up the gallows to be hanged again. Then, to serve as a warning to others, Kidd's body was smothered in tar, wrapped in chains, and left to rot in public view.

> **"I have lodged goods and treasures to the value of 100,000 pounds in the Indies."**
> **William Kidd**

Hubert Palmer knew that as a group, pirates tended to be spenders rather than savers. Most squandered their money while in port, knowing full well that they could get more when they set out for sea once again. But William Kidd was an exception to the rule. He had bragged openly about his secret hoards. He even wrote about them. Shortly before his execution, Kidd sent a plea-bargaining letter to the governor stating: "I have lodged goods and treasures to the value of 100,000 pounds in the Indies."

With the promise of treasure in mind, Palmer searched the desk each evening, always hopeful that within its secret drawers and compartments, he would find clues to Kidd's missing fortune.

One evening, as Palmer made his usual examination of the desk, he discovered a lump in the wood. Using a knife he dug out

Chapter 1 ~ **PIRATE TREASURE**

a plug and behind it, in a hollow cavity, found a brass tube containing a tightly rolled sheet of parchment. It was a map, showing an island in a bay, surrounded by reefs and dotted with trees. Trails crisscrossed the island, the number of paces of each printed alongside. The words *China Sea* were scrawled across the top and at the bottom *W.K. 1669.* There was a compass drawing showing north, and nearby the words: *of me Sarah-W.*

China Sea? Palmer knew that Kidd had roamed the Western Indian Ocean, terrorizing merchant ships that sailed those waters. At some point, it was said, Kidd had put ashore on an island near the coast of Madagascar to divide the booty with his crew. Did the map show the location of the pirate's buried treasure?

The island had an unusual shape, unlike any found on other maps or charts. Try as he might, Palmer could not figure out the island's exact location. Was the map genuine or a clever forgery?

Palmer searched for other Kidd relics. He advertised in a newspaper and in 1931 received word from an antique dealer that an oak chest once belonging to Captain Kidd had been located. Was Palmer interested? In no time, Palmer was at the dealer's shop, breathless with anticipation.

The chest came with a note from Captain Dan Morgan, a collector of antiques. It said: *As you seem keen for pirate stuff i have dug something out of my attik wich may sute you it is a bit more Kidd stuff and hope you will like it . . .*

The chest certainly looked old enough to have been Kidd's. A skull and crossbones was carved on the lid and the monogram *K* was engraved on a brass plate. A bit of research revealed that it had once belonged to Ned Ward, one of Kidd's shipmates. Ward, it seemed, had inherited the chest from Kidd himself and somehow over the years it had come into Captain Morgan's possession.

Palmer bought the heavy chest and lugged it home. Each evening he dragged it to the centre of his study and examined it carefully. If Kidd had hidden a map in the desk, could he not have done the same to the chest? Palmer tapped the sides, pulled on boards, and ran his fingers along the bumps and curves of the wood.

One night, Palmer found a few protruding nails on the bottom. They were, in fact, cleverly disguised screws, and once removed, revealed a false bottom. Attached to it was a slim book and behind that another map, identical in almost every way to the first. Along the edge of the map were the words: *The path*

Hubert Palmer holds the false bottom of the chest in which a concealed map was found.

Chapter 1 ~ PIRATE TREASURE

that must be followed to find my treasure, Captain William Kidd 1691.

Once again, Palmer inspected maps of the Western Indian Ocean, checking known islands, looking for clues to the treasure's whereabouts. Once again, he fell short. Nothing matched the island's shape or description.

Over the next few years, other objects belonging to Captain Kidd found their way into Palmer's possession. He was offered another chest and a small box believed to have belonged to Kidd's wife, Sarah. These held maps, too, showing the same strange island, the identical trails, the exact same trees.

One of the chests bore the names of not only William Kidd, but also Sarah Kidd. The map inside was the most detailed and bore geographical markings giving the island's location. Unfortunately, these proved to be old methods of plotting position, quite different from those used on modern maps. Once again, the clues proved impossible to follow. Try as he might, Palmer had reached a dead end.

News of Palmer's discoveries spread, awakening interest in the old maps. Treasure hunters approached Palmer, anxious to study the maps themselves. Some claimed to recognize the island, saying they knew where it was. Deals were pitched, sailing ventures planned.

Palmer seemed to be on the verge of finalizing arrangements for a treasure-hunting expedition when he died in 1949. The maps passed on to his housekeeper, Elizabeth Dick. For a time she entertained the idea of launching her own expedition. Then she gave up the plan and, in need of money, tried selling the maps instead.

Where are the maps today? In 1957 Mrs. Dick sold the maps to a syndicate of Canadian and American treasure seekers. A Mr. Maurice Taylor of Toronto, Ontario, apparently served as the contact person for the group and, when last seen, the four

charts and various other items from Palmer's collection were in his possession.

That is where the trail runs cold. The maps simply vanished and with them all traces of Taylor. The island has never been found. Captain Kidd's treasure, if there is one, still lies buried.

Were the maps truly genuine? Were they really the work of Kidd himself, clever forgeries of a skilled artist from the 1600s, or an immense practical joke played by Hubert Palmer, a respected British lawyer?

No one really knows.

A similar map was found in yet another, smaller chest that Palmer acquired.

Lost & Found
Pirate Treasure

Lost: Great Treasure of Lima

In 1820, with invading forces on their doorstep, Spanish officials in Lima, Peru, hatched a wild plan to protect their city's gold and silver treasures. They entrusted them to a British sea captain named William Thompson, a well-known trader in the area. With the treasure aboard his ship, the *Mary Dear*, Thompson was to sail the ocean for several months until the situation in Lima improved.

Once Thompson was out of sight of land, however, he and his crew massacred the guards who had been sent along, tossed their bodies overboard and set sail for Cocos, a tiny island 560 kilometres southeast of Costa Rica. There they unloaded and buried the treasure.

Later the *Mary Dear* was captured by the Spanish. To save their lives, Thompson and his first mate struck a deal, promising to lead their captors to the treasure. But once on the island, the two escaped, disappearing into the jungle, never to be seen again.

The Great Treasure of Lima is said to be worth $100 million or more. Although there have been more than three hundred treasure-seeking expeditions to the island, the treasure has never been found. Likely that's the way it will remain. In order to protect the island as a wildlife refuge, the Costa Rican government no longer grants licences for treasure hunting on Cocos.

Lost: **Jonathan Lambert's Hoard**

In 1811 pirate Jonathan Lambert and his crew took possession of the island of Tristan in the South Atlantic. They stashed their goods there and used the island as the base for their operations. But the plan soon turned sour. Lambert and all but one of his men died shortly after, victims it seems to a mishap at sea.

When British troops arrived in 1816, they found only one survivor — a chatty, rum-drinking sailor named Thomas Currie, who seemed to have an endless supply of mysterious gold coins. He told the troops about a buried treasure hidden "between two waterfalls," and promised to lead them to it. Unfortunately Currie died of a stroke, and the hoard's location died with him. Despite many attempts, the treasure has never been found — and the chances of finding it now are slim. In 1961 a volcano erupted on the island, sealing the treasure — if there was one — under a mountain of lava.

Found: **Port Royal**

In 1965 Robert Marx, the archaeologist who helped identify the *Santa Maria de la Consolacion*, excavated a sunken city off the coast of Jamaica. The city was Port Royal, a pirate hideaway that was swallowed by the ocean after a violent earthquake in 1692. Among the many treasures recovered was a chest containing hundreds of gold coins. Historians believe the chest may have belonged to the pirate Henry Morgan. A ruthless leader, Morgan organized fellow pirates into a powerful army and led them in carefully plotted raids against Spanish settlements in the Caribbean, capturing entire cities and amassing a vast fortune. The treasure chest may have been part of an immense hoard hidden by Morgan in the doomed city.

Believed Found: The *Adventure Galley*

In 2000 divers led by Barry Clifford, who discovered the *Whydah*, found the remains of a wooden ship in the harbour of Ste. Marie, a small island off Madagascar. The wreck may be the *Adventure Galley*, the ship used by pirate captain William Kidd from 1696 to 1698. The location of the wreck matches the last known whereabouts of the galley, but the most convincing proof comes from an unusual object pulled from the sea — a metal oarlock 30 centimetres long. Most ships of Kidd's time were equipped only with sails. The *Adventure Galley*, however, was a true galley, having not only sails but oars. That way, when the wind failed, Kidd could charge ahead, overtaking sailing vessels stranded on the calm sea.

Believed Found: The *Queen Anne's Revenge*

In 1996 divers discovered a huge mound of cannons, anchors, ballast stones and thousands of artifacts under 6 metres of water near Beaufort Inlet, North Carolina. Evidence suggests it is the wreck of the *Queen Anne's Revenge*, the flagship of Blackbeard's fleet. The ship ran aground and sank while Blackbeard, a brutal pirate who harassed ships along the Atlantic coast of North America, was entering the inlet in the summer of 1718.

Today divers and archaeologists still work the site, hopeful they will uncover new information about pirates and their ways. Their work grows more urgent with each passing day. When the ship sank three hundred years ago, it became buried under almost 5 metres of sand. Now, because of storms, only 1 metre of sand covers and protects the wreck. Each new storm threatens to destroy more of the ship and sweep valuable artifacts away.

Chapter 2
OVERLOOKED TREASURE

In Their Own Words

"Dear Mr. Smith . . . had the most queer-looking specimen brought to notice yesterday . . . "
Marjorie Courtenay Latimer, describing an odd creature pulled from the sea

"It didn't look very special. How wrong we were."
John Lever, headmaster of Canford School, describing a three-thousand-year-old carving discovered in the school cafeteria

"I was about to get rid of all of it because it was so nasty . . . "
Ron Hamilton, clothing expert, on coming close to tossing aside a treasure worth more than US$46,000

"Shouldn't it be yellow?"
Fourteen-year-old Georg Wilhelm Backman, wondering about an unusual stamp in his collection

"I couldn't keep my eyes off it . . . I was sure it was old."
Ten-year-old Bingham Bryant, describing what was special about a grime-covered painting in his school library

"It was like a dream come true. It was like winning the lottery."
Bill Moorehouse, expressing his reaction to an unexpected discovery inside the walls of his home

Chapter 2 ~ OVERLOOKED TREASURE

 East London Museum, East London, South Africa

A Living Fossil

Beneath a pile of fish, Marjorie Courtenay Latimer spotted a shiny blue fin. Immediately, she sensed the fish was special, a treasure if there ever was one.

When Captain Hendrick Goosen of the trawler *Nerine* pulled into East London, South Africa, on December 23, 1938, he phoned Marjorie Courtenay Latimer, the curator of the tiny East London Museum. He had fish aboard the trawler. Would Latimer like to look through them?

Always interested in acquiring new specimens for the museum, thirty-two-year-old Latimer often met Goosen at the docks to look through his catch. But on this day she hesitated. She was preparing a reptile collection for display and was eager to finish the job. Still, Latimer reminded herself, it was close to Christmas — she should at least drop by and wish the captain and his crew well.

Latimer took a taxi to the docks, stopped to deliver her message, and was about to leave when she noticed something unusual in the pile of fish nearby. Beneath the manta rays, groupers and sharks, wedged between drab shades of grey, she spotted a shiny blue fin. It caught the light, glistening like a rare jewel among the more common varieties.

Latimer pushed aside the other fish and dug deep into the pile. What she saw took her breath away. "It was the most beautiful fish I had ever seen," she wrote later, "five feet long and a pale mauve blue with iridescent markings."

The fish was also incredibly odd. It was heavily armoured

and covered with thick scales. Its fins were thick, sturdy and almost leg-like, not delicate like those of most fish.

Whatever is this? wondered Latimer. Never before had she seen a specimen quite like it. Sensing that the fish was special, she decided to take it to the museum. It would make a wonderful addition to her collections.

The coelacanth, long thought to be extinct. Note the unusual fins.

The taxi driver had other plans. He refused to let the smelly creature in his cab. The two argued. In the end the taxi driver relented and drove Latimer and her catch back to the museum.

Latimer knew that the fish would deteriorate quickly in the relentless South African heat. The museum lacked refrigeration equipment, so she began a desperate search. She loaded the carcass onto an old wooden trolley and wheeled it through the streets of East London, first to the local city morgue and then to a cold-storage centre. At each location she struck out.

In the end she carted the fish back to the museum. Time was running out. Only one option remained. With the help of the museum's taxidermist, the fish was sliced open, its innards were removed, and the fish was mounted, its skin and skeleton preserved and intact.

Latimer dove into reference books, flipping pages, eager to find an illustration of the unusual fish. Only one remotely matched — a prehistoric creature known to science only through fossils. Impossible, Latimer thought. Or was it? The creature in the book had been extinct for *millions* of years. Yet here was a real fish, blue, gnarled and similar in many respects to the long-extinct one.

Eager for answers, Latimer made a sketch of the fish, labelled its parts and fired off a letter to accompany it. *Dear Mr. Smith*, it began, *I had the most queer-looking specimen brought to notice yesterday* . . . She sent the letter to James Leonard Smith, a chemistry teacher and fish expert at Rhodes University. Smith was away on holidays, and it wasn't until early January that Latimer received his reply by telegram:

MOST IMPORTANT PRESERVE SKELETON AND GILLS OF FISH DESCRIBED.

It was too late. In the rush to preserve the fish, the internal organs had been tossed away. Despite a frantic search of the museum's trash bins, the insides of the fish could not be found.

When Smith finally arrived at the East London Museum several weeks later, the mounted carcass was all that remained. But that was enough to satisfy his curiosity and provide him with the information he needed. After careful examination he identified the fish as a coelacanth (SEE-la-canth), a creature that was thought to have disappeared some 65 million years ago.

The news stunned the world of science. Finding a live specimen of an ancient, long-extinct fish was about the same as finding a dinosaur romping in a school playground. Both seemed impossible. But here it was . . . a real specimen from the distant past. A living fossil. Suddenly the impossible seemed very possible.

Most puzzling to scientists were the coelacanth's unusual fins. The thick, knobby fins, some believed, were signs of evolution at work.

According to evolutional theory, life started in the ocean. Eventually, as creatures evolved, some left their watery surroundings, developing legs and lungs that enabled them to live on land. Was the coelacanth a missing link? Was it a creature poised to leave the ocean, a forerunner to animals that eventually did live on land? Perhaps.

Other coelacanths were later found, all in an isolated stretch of South Africa's waters. Then, in 1997, another specimen was found on a fish cart in a market on the Indonesian island of Sulawesi, 10,000 kilometres from the Comoros Islands. It provided clues to a second habitat where coelacanth flourished.

The discovery was called the find of the twentieth century. It fuelled hot debate and raised many questions. How had the fish survived extinction? How had it escaped notice for so long? Were there others just like it? Where?

In time other specimens of "old four legs" — Smith's nickname for the rare fish — were discovered and studied. With each find, some questions have been answered while new ones have surfaced to take their place. For scientists, the coelacanth still remains a rare, mysterious and fascinating creature.

Marjorie Courtenay Latimer lived on in East London, studying the natural world and its many treasures, until her death in 2004 at the age of 97. A coelacanth is still on display in the very museum where Latimer once worked. Mounted and preserved, blue and iridescent, it is reminder to the rest of us that the meaning of treasure — like beauty itself — is all in the eye of the beholder.

"But It's Yellow!"

One stamp caught the fourteen-year-old boy's attention. It was familiar, yet somehow different, too.

Georg Wilhelm Backman crawled past boxes, heaps of clothing and chipped furniture, all old and dusty. The fourteen-year-old Swedish boy was in his grandmother's attic during the Christmas holidays in 1885, searching for a dresser bureau. Tucked inside one of the drawers, his grandmother promised, Georg would find what he was looking for.

Georg had been collecting stamps for a while, but he was always on the lookout for new ones. That was the reason he was in the attic — to check the letters his grandmother stored there, to find stamps to add to his collection.

Inside one bureau Georg found old letters, bundled and tied together, still in their original envelopes, just as his grandmother said they would be. He flipped through the envelopes, his eyes scanning the upper right corner of each one.

One stamp caught his attention. It was familiar, yet somehow different, too. The odd-looking stamp was a Three Skilling Banco, a fairly ordinary stamp issued in 1857. Normally, the stamp was blue-green in colour. This one was yellow. Georg had never seen a yellow Three Skilling Banco.

With his grandmother's permission, Georg removed the stamp from the envelope. When he returned home to Stockholm, he took it to a stamp dealer named Heinrich Lichtenstein. Georg had heard that Lichtenstein was buying Three Skilling Bancos and that he paid up to 7 Swedish *kronor* for each one (about half a dollar at the time).

Lichtenstein examined the stamp carefully. He seemed surprised. "But it's *yellow!*" Georg reportedly heard him mumble over and over. Georg grew uneasy. Was there something wrong?

"Shouldn't it be yellow?" he asked.

"No," the dealer replied. "It should be green."

Now Georg was worried. Thoughts of newfound riches vanished. "Will you pay me 7 *kronor* or not?" he asked.

"I will pay the 7 *kronor* even though it is yellow," Lichtenstein replied.

Georg was relieved. Seven *kronor* for a discoloured stamp? What a deal!

It *was* a deal . . . for Lichtenstein. The stamp was an oddity, a one-of-a-kind fluke. That made it very rare — and valuable.

Lichtenstein sold the stamp to a Vienna dealer, who in turn sold it for a higher price to another collector. Since that time, the Three Skilling Yellow, as the stamp is called, has changed hands many times. With each exchange, the stamp has climbed in value. In 1937 it sold for US$30,000. In 1984 it sold for more than half a million dollars. In 1990 it set a world record, selling for more than US$1 million. This was topped in 1996, when it was reportedly sold again for US$2.3 million.

Since its discovery in 1885, the stamp's authenticity has been questioned. Some experts believe the stamp is a fake, that perhaps bleach was used to alter the stamp's normal colour after it was issued, and that the story of its discovery is a lie. Most, though, believe the stamp is genuine. Its yellow colour, they argue, is the result of a printing error. Instead of using blue-green ink during production, the printer accidentally used yellow ink and the stamp was simply released by mistake. Scientific tests conducted on the stamp support this last view.

The stamp, with a cancellation mark across it.

Stored and Forgotten

One of a Kind

In 1873 twelve-year-old Vernon Vaughan, a Scottish boy, discovered a British Guiana one-cent stamp on one of his uncle's letters stored in an attic. The octagonal stamp was printed in black ink on magenta paper. The ink was smudged, and the stamp was dirty and heavily postmarked. Vernon soaked the stamp, peeled it loose and kept it in his album with his other stamps. Thinking it unattractive, he later sold it to a local collector for 6 shillings (at that time less than US$1.00).

That "dirty" stamp is considered by many to be the world's rarest stamp. Called the British Guiana One Cent Magenta, the stamp is the only known one of its kind. In 1980 it was auctioned for US$935,000.

Home Run

In 1996, when schoolboy Chris Scala chose baseball great Babe Ruth as his subject for a school dress-up project, his great-grandmother, Viola Bevilaque, found something to go with Chris's outfit — a long-forgotten ball with Ruth's signature on it. The baseball had been stored in a box in her attic along with other things belonging to her husband, who had been given the ball in 1927. An inscription inside the box proved that the baseball was the very first one hit by Ruth for a home run in Yankee Stadium. In 1998 the ball sold at auction for US$126,500.

Cooper-Hewitt National Design Museum,
New York City, New York

Box 366 — More Than Just Light Bulbs

In April 2002 Sir Timothy Clifford, a Scottish art scholar, spent a week in the fourth-floor storeroom of the Cooper-Hewitt Museum in New York City, inspecting dozens of boxes. He was searching for uncatalogued art — pieces bypassed or missed by others — but so far had not had much luck. Box 366, labelled "lighting fixtures," promised nothing out of the ordinary, either. Clifford expected to find sketches of lamps and chandeliers inside.

Tucked in the box, along with drawings by unknown artists, he found one that was truly special — a rare, unsigned black chalk and brown wash drawing by Michelangelo Buonarroti, the famous sixteenth-century Italian artist. Buonarroti had sculpted the statue of David which stands in Florence, Italy, painted the ceiling of the Sistine Chapel in the Vatican, and was responsible for dozens of other renowned works of art. The drawing of an elaborate seven-branched candlestick or menorah, which had been stored and forgotten in the box for over sixty years, was valued at over $10 million.

Coin in a Can

An old Prince Albert tobacco can sat in a New York state home for generations, ignored and hardly ever opened. When the owner died in 1976, his son opened the lid and discovered a dozen coins. One, chocolate brown in colour and the size of a quarter, was stamped *1792*. Interesting, the man thought, but not noteworthy. He closed the lid and for many years kept the can in a small living-room safe.

In 2004 family members, acting on a hunch, brought the coin to a coin collectors' show in Pittsburgh. The coin, it turned out, was a 1792 American copper penny, one of only nine in existence. "It's like the Holy Grail just showed up on our doorstep," coin expert Kenneth Bressett said of the discovery. In 2005 the rare penny was auctioned for US$437,000.

Here's to You

Beer mugs are fairly common. Two-hundred-and-sixty-year-old silver ones are rarer and more valuable. But a silver tankard made in 1742 and engraved with the letters *GAO* tops them all. Its estimated value is $100,000. The reason? The tangled story behind the beer mug, among other things.

The elaborately engraved tankard was made in 1742 as a wedding gift for a Philadelphia couple, George and Anne Okill; it bore their initials *GAO*. From there, it passed to their daughter, Jane, and her husband, Rev. John Stuart. During the American Revolution, the Stuarts remained loyal to Britain. Rebels looted and burned their home and the Stuarts, fearing for their lives, escaped to Canada, taking the tankard with them. Rev. Stuart became a leading churchman in Upper Canada and eventually the tankard was inherited by their son, Sir James Stuart, who served as a prominent chief justice of Quebec. When his three sons died without heirs, the tankard was placed in a London bank vault for safekeeping in 1908. There it was forgotten until it was rediscovered in 1969.

The tankard's excellent condition, its well-documented journey, and its passage from one famous hand to another — all of these factors contributed to its value.

Just Filthy

The pants were ripped, caked with mud and in terrible condition, but they were worth a fortune.

In 1998 a young truck driver was passing through an abandoned mining town in central Nevada when he stopped to explore its homesteads and crumbling buildings. Inside one shack he spotted some broken tools and a box of old clothing.

Just junk, the man thought. Leave it.

But then he reconsidered. His parents were friends of Ron Hamilton, who owned a dry goods store in Kentucky. Hamilton, an expert on vintage clothing, was always on the lookout for old, unusual, one-of-a-kind items. The truck driver scooped up the box, loaded it in his truck, drove off and later shipped it to Hamilton.

In the box Hamilton found some shirts, a coat, shoes, a pair of pants and a few rocks. The clothes were caked with mud and coated with grime, tattered, worn and barely recognizable. "I was about to get rid of all of it because it was so nasty," Hamilton said later, "but at the last moment I decided I would wash the pants."

It took five cycles in the washing machine to flush out layers of dirt. The mud-caked pants, though ripped and faded, emerged clean. They were actually blue in colour, not brown.

Blue jeans, Hamilton realized. He recognized the style and make. Levi's jeans. Very *old* Levi's jeans.

But just how old were they? And were they valuable?

Hamilton contacted Levi Strauss & Co. Founded in 1853, the company had been producing jeans of all types and styles since 1873. Levi Strauss & Co. also had a museum that showcased its clothing collection, and the company employed historians and archivists to maintain it.

Chapter 2 ~ OVERLOOKED TREASURE

Over the phone Hamilton described the jeans to one of the historians. Each detail provided clues to the jeans' age and origin.

"There's one back pocket," he said.

"That makes it 1901 or earlier," the historian explained. After that date, all jeans had two back pockets.

"They also have a side pocket, something like a tool pocket found on workpants."

There was a lull in the conversation. The company, the historian explained, had no record of jeans with *side* pockets. As it turned out, during the 1906 San Francisco earthquake, the Levi Strauss & Co. building had been destroyed. Records of pants before that date had been lost in a fire, and the company couldn't verify the age of the jeans over the phone. They *were* Levi's jeans and they *were* old, but just how old no one there could say for certain.

Hamilton took the jeans to Zip Stevenson, a denim expert and clothing restorer in Los Angeles. He inspected the pants, noting their unique stitching, the rivets along the pockets, the unusual tool pocket. His excitement grew as he realized how special the jeans were.

"Man, these are amazing," he said. "I've never even heard people talk about this existing. This jean is like a hundred and twenty years old. Yep, this is the oldest pair of Levi's. I'm confident of it."

His hunch proved correct. When the jeans were later examined by Lynn Downey, the historian for Levi Strauss & Co., she confirmed their age, dating them to the mid–1880s. Hamilton auctioned the jeans on eBay in 2001, with the winning bid of US$46,532 going to the company that had made the pants more than a century before — Levi Strauss & Co. The pants were christened the Nevada Jean in honour of where they were found.

Although Hamilton received the money, the truck driver

| 1880s miner | 1900s cowboy | Today's style |

When the vintage jeans were first worn, probably in the mid-1880s, Canada was barely a teenager, the United States was just over a hundred years old, and your great-great-grandfather probably wasn't even born yet. Miners often wore jeans because of denim's sturdiness.

who found the jeans was rewarded, too. When the jeans were first identified, he struck a deal with Ron Hamilton. In exchange for the old, tattered jeans — now Hamilton's to do with as he pleased — the young man would receive a lifetime supply of new jeans, his to select from the store as he wished. It was an arrangement that suited them both.

Today, the Nevada Jean is locked in a fireproof safe in the company's San Francisco archives, protected from dirt and harm, a treasured piece of company history.

*Chapter 2 ~ **OVERLOOKED TREASURE***

Treasure Tips

People collect all kind of things: stamps, coins, comic books, baseball cards, dolls, CDs, toys . . . Objects like these that are collected for pleasure or for profit are called *collectibles*.

Collectibles become valuable when other people save the same objects and are willing to purchase new ones to add to their collections. A collectible's value is determined by its condition, the number of people who are interested in having the object, and the number of objects that are in circulation. Collectibles that are in excellent condition and in high demand, but are also not very plentiful, usually fetch the highest prices.

To check the value of an object in your collection, you might try the Internet. There are many websites devoted to collectibles. A number of these sites list items for sale. By comparing the asking price and condition of these articles, you can get a rough idea of the value of your own.

"I Was Sure It Was Old"

During English class, Bingham Bryant's attention wandered to the dingy painting in the school library. Was it really a masterpiece, as he suspected?

Ten-year-old Bingham Bryant stared at the unframed painting propped up on a bookcase behind the librarian's desk. The painting was old. No one would deny that. It had been in the library of Old Lyme Central School in Connecticut for almost eighty years. During that time, thousands of students had hurried past it, barely giving it a glance. On occasion, when a teacher wanted to illustrate a point about art or Greek mythology, it was hauled off the bookcase and passed from student to student. Mostly, though, the painting was ignored.

> **The painting was choked with dirt and smothered by layers of varnish.**

The painting depicted a story from Greek mythology — the god Hades and two black stallions emerging from the underworld to kidnap the maiden Persephone. The painting was choked with dirt and smothered by layers of varnish. Its colours were muted, dim and dingy. It was as if someone inside the painting had turned out the lights, throwing the scene into darkness.

Bingham knew a thing or two about art. His father, Christopher, was an antique dealer, and the family collected keepsakes from the past. Despite the painting's gloom, there was something about it that appealed to Bingham. During English class one day in 2000, he stared at it long and hard.

"I couldn't keep my eyes off it," he admitted later. "I'm interested in Greek mythology and very classical painting. I was sure it was old. I just wasn't sure if it was good or no[t]."

Bingham told his father about the painting. His enthusiasm

convinced Christopher Bryant to visit the school and see the picture for himself. It was everything his son had described — elegant lines, dramatic presentation, classical subject — all the hallmarks of a masterpiece.

"I realized as soon as I saw it that it was something quite special and quite wonderful," Bryant said.

Father and son dug into the painting's past. They searched through art books looking for references to it. To their surprise they discovered that it was the work of famous British artist Walter Crane. The painting had a name, *The Fate of Persephone*, but the last time it had been seen was in Germany in 1923.

How did a genuine Crane get to be in a school library in the United States? More research revealed the painting's unusual past and a story as fascinating as the discovery itself.

Walter Crane lived during the late 1800s and early 1900s. He was regarded as a revolutionary painter, known for his experimental designs with various media. In 1878 Crane painted *The Fate of Persephone*. It was sold several times, but in 1923 it was purchased by Brian Hooker, a university professor. Hooker hoped to hang the painting in a house he was planning on building. In the meantime he lent it to Old Lyme Central School. Hooker never reclaimed it, and by the time he died in 1966, the painting's history was forgotten.

Who rightfully owned the painting now? Christopher Bryant did more digging. He tracked down Hooker's heirs — two surviving daughters, both in their eighties. Legally, the painting was theirs. They agreed to sell it.

The painting was cleaned. With years of neglect removed,

In *The Fate of Persephone*, the maiden is stolen away from her friends and carried off to the underworld.

its true colours and delicate lines were revealed. Art experts examined the piece and verified its authenticity. On June 12, 2002, the painting was put up for auction. The bidding was lively, the interest in the painting high. When the gavel came down, the painting sold for £424,650.

Thanks to Bingham Bryant, whose attention wandered during English class, the rare painting has been rescued and restored to its former glory.

Treasure Tips

Not sure if a painting is valuable? Most artists sign their work. Often they date it, too. The name and the date on the painting can be the first clues to a painting's worth. By doing a web search and by checking art catalogues, it's possible to find out if the artist is well known, if the painting is listed or described, and what its value might be.

Surprise Masterpieces

More Junk?

What? More junk? That was the reaction of Carl Rice's wife when he brought home a handful of paintings purchased at an estate sale in Tucson, Arizona, on a Saturday in 1996. One painting, bought for $10, was a small picture of some roses. Another, a painting of magnolia blossoms, cost Carl $50.

When the Rices looked more closely, they found the initials *M.J.H.* on one of the pieces. With a little research, they discovered that the artist — Martin Johnson Heade — was a well-known nineteenth-century painter. The two paintings were auctioned in 1998 for more than US$1 million. Afterwards, the original owners sued the Rices, claiming that the paintings had been sold by mistake. The Rices eventually won the case and kept the proceeds.

Just Hanging Around

A couple who bought a ramshackle Ontario farmhouse in 1973 got more than they expected. Figuring that a painting that hung on one wall looked "nice," they negotiated with the seller to have it left behind. The painting, which showed two young women gathering flowers in a meadow, hung in the home for more than twenty-five years. In 2001, when the couple decided to sell it, they got the surprise of their lives. The painting, titled *Gather ye Rosebuds while ye may*, was a lost work by John William Waterhouse, a famous British artist. Its value? As much as $7.3 million, some experts say.

Chapter 2 ~ **OVERLOOKED TREASURE**

A Real Bargain

Although the picture was pretty, it was the frame that caught the eye of Jean Comey-Smith as she browsed through a thrift shop in Fort Myers, Florida, in 1998. Then, when she flipped the picture over, she spotted something else — the name *A. Rodin*. Could this be a work by *the* Auguste Rodin, the famous French artist? Comey-Smith wondered. "I thought, 'I couldn't be that lucky. It's got to be a copy. It's got to be a print.'" For $1.99 — the price on the painting — Comey-Smith bought the picture, then left it in her car for nearly a month before checking her hunch. Experts verified that it was an original Rodin and estimated it to be worth at least US$14,000.

 National Gallery of Ireland, Dublin, Ireland

Mistaken Identity

In 1990 art historian Sergio Benedetti was called to a Dublin home for Jesuit priests to check out a dingy painting that had hung in the dining room for sixty years. Although a plaque at the bottom identified the painting as *The Betrayal of Christ* by Gerard Honthorst, Benedetti felt the style, colours and subject matched a different artist. After some investigation Benedetti identified the painting as *The Taking of Christ* by Michelangelo Merisi da Caravaggio, a famous seventeenth-century Italian artist. Because Caravaggio paintings are rare, some experts estimate this one could be worth more than US$40 million.

The painting is on loan to Ireland's National Gallery. Recently some art historians have claimed that another painting discovered in Rome is the original *Taking of Christ*, not the Dublin one.

 Miho Museum, Shiga, Japan

Older Than the School Itself

The mural hung in the school cafeteria, wedged between the dartboard and candy dispenser. No one recognized it for the ancient treasure it was.

Hungry students munched on pizza and downed soft drinks in the "Grubber," the cafeteria of Canford School in Dorset, England. To pass the time, they fired darts at a dartboard on the wall. Sometimes the darts strayed, hitting a plaster mural instead, punching pinprick holes in its surface.

The mural was a fixture in the Grubber. It had been there forever, it seemed, along a wall between the dartboard and candy dispenser and directly across from a pop machine and the pizza counter. Egyptian-like carvings covered the mural, making it look precious and old. But as everyone at Canford knew, the mural was just a plaster replica, a cheap copy of something ancient and original. So whenever the mural became dirty, smudged with fingerprints or pocked with too many holes, it was simply slathered with a fresh coat of paint.

Canford School has an unusual history. Built in the 1800s, it was the home of a wealthy family for many years. Later an addition was built. A relative of the family had returned from Mesopotamia (now Iraq), bringing several enormous three-thousand-year-old stone panels from the ruins of the ancient Assyrian city of Nineveh. The panels were installed in the addition, making an elaborate mural along one wall. In the 1920s

Chapter 2 ~ **OVERLOOKED TREASURE**

the home was sold and converted to Canford School, and the addition became the Grubber, the cafeteria. The panels were dismantled and carted off to the Metropolitan Museum of Art in New York City, and plaster reproductions were installed in their place.

Or so everyone thought.

In 1993 John Russell, a professor at Columbia University in New York City, paid a visit to the school. He was writing a book about the Assyrian panels in the Metropolitan Museum and wanted to see the place where they had originally stood. As soon as Russell stepped into the cafeteria, he noticed that something was out of place.

"Inside the door on the right wall were still some plaster casts and that was wonderful, but there was one I didn't recognize. It wasn't a cast of a known piece."

The centre slab depicted a royal figure and a bearded, winged god. The slab was covered with several thick coats of paint, smothering its fine lines and obscuring the details. Pinpricks from misfired darts dotted the surface. Was this an original carving?

Russell moved in for a closer look. Some of the paint was scraped away. Underneath Russell found marble, not plaster. It was the type of marble that came from distant places, a match to the marble used on the panels housed in the Metropolitan Museum. The slab was authentic — a three-thousand-year-old carving from an Assyrian palace. Somehow it had been left behind when the others had been dismantled and replaced with plaster copies.

John Lever, the school's headmaster, described the new-found panel this way: "It didn't look very special. How wrong we were. But once it was cleaned up you could see it far better and

you do begin to stand and stare and wonder. It is a fairly remarkable thing now, but you can imagine it covered in peeling paint, it wasn't special at all."

According to British law, the panel rightfully belonged to the school. On July 6, 1994, it was put up for auction. The school hoped the Assyrian panel would sell for as high as a million pounds. Bidding was fierce. Offers flew across the room, and in just five minutes, the auction was over. The panel was sold to the Miho Museum in Japan for £7,701,500, making it the world's most valuable art antiquity at the time.

The students at Canford School are the real winners. With money from the auction, the school has started a scholarship fund and constructed a new theatre, sports centre and boarding houses.

The Assyrian panel, freed from its coat of paint.

Treasure in Unlikely Places

Stuck Under the Sofa

When book specialist Simon Roberts was appraising the books and the furniture in a Suffolk, England, home in 1996, he discovered a large album inside a pouch. On its first page, he found a sheet of paper covered in elegant handwriting that he recognized as that of George Washington, the first United States president. The sheet was a page from Washington's inaugural speech delivered on April 30, 1789. The document sold at auction for US$275,000.

Bottom of the Box

Don Troiani of Southbury, Connecticut, went to an auction in 1996 hoping to find some rare clothing to add to his collection. A box of World War II uniforms caught his eye, but at first Troiani was tempted to pass them by. Such uniforms were fairly common and not what he was after. Nevertheless Troiani dug through the box, hopeful that other treasures might be hidden inside. At the bottom he found a green sharpshooter's uniform from the American Civil War. It was extremely rare, in excellent condition and exactly what Troiani wanted. He got the whole box of uniforms for US$325. At the time the Civil War uniform had an estimated value of US$30,000–$50,000.

Stuffed in the Walls

When a huge storm hit Three Oaks, Michigan, in 1992, the rain seeped through the leaky roof of an old home just purchased by Bill Moorehouse and Joseph Foxhood. The water ran down the walls, soaking into the plaster and ruining the finish. When workers tore down the plaster, they discovered thousands of old movie posters — sometimes five or six deep — that had been stuffed into the walls.

In the 1930s the house had belonged to the manager of the local movie theatre. Each day he had brought home discarded posters to use as insulation in the walls. The entire collection was valued at hundreds of thousands of dollars. "It was like a dream come true. It was like winning the lottery," Moorehouse said.

 Henry Ford Museum, Dearborn, Michigan

Junkyard Gold

In 1943, when Charles Chayne found a rusting hulk of a car in a wrecking yard, he saw an opportunity others had missed. The old wreck was a Type 41 Bugatti Royale, an extremely rare, unique and majestic car that was produced in France in 1930. Only six had been built and none of the six was exactly like the others. Chayne purchased the car for US$412, repaired and restored it, then, in 1958 donated it to the Henry Ford Museum. Bugatti Royales are among the world's most valuable cars. In 1990 another Bugatti Royale sold for a cool US$15 million, a world record at the time.

Chapter 3
SUNKEN TREASURE

In Their Own Words

"Glittering, tinkling coins danced around in my head for hours. My dream — my lifelong dream — was being realized. We had found treasure, and we had found it right where I knew it had to be all these years."

Kip Wagner, upon finding a ship from a Spanish fleet that sank in 1715

"Well, boss, I've got good news and bad news. The bad news is that I just tore up your net. The good news is that I just made the best catch of my life."

Jerry Murphy, telling his uncle of a surprising discovery at sea

"Just wait until you see the main pile. There'll be stacks of silver bars lined up like a brick wall on the ocean floor. There'll be bars of gold and treasure chests filled with gold and silver coins. It's all there. Believe me."

Mel Fisher, to his crew just before finding the Atocha, *the world's richest Spanish shipwreck*

"No diving adventure anywhere compares with the excitement of uncovering a beautiful object that nobody has seen for twenty-six hundred years."

Gian Luigi Sacco, diver on the Giglio wreck

 McLarty Museum, St. Sebastian, Florida

Finding the Lost Fleet

When Kip Wagner rubbed the blackened object, he felt a jolt of surprise. His eye caught a glint of silver. Then a date appeared — 1714!

Kip Wagner struggled across the beach near Sebastian Inlet, fighting the wild wind and the wet sand that slowed his every step. A hurricane had pounded the Florida coast, tearing bluffs apart, shifting sand, re-sculpting the shoreline. As a volunteer with a local disaster unit, Wagner had a job to do. Examine the beach. Check for erosion after the storm. Make sure cottages were safe and secure.

Wagner was familiar with this beach. Although he was a building contractor by trade, the sea was his first love. He had visited this stretch of beach along the Atlantic Ocean many times before and knew every bump and curve. But on this day in the late 1950s, the beach bore little resemblance to the one Wagner knew so well. The storm had changed everything. Sand covered well-travelled trails. Palm trees leaned at awkward angles. Seaweed and driftwood littered the shore.

After checking the cottages for damage, Wagner was walking close to the water's edge when he spotted something in the sand. It had the faint gleam of metal and was obviously not a seashell or other natural object. When he picked it up he felt a jolt of surprise.

It was a coin. Tarnished, crusted with sea growth, irregularly shaped and barely recognizable. But it was a coin — a Spanish one, and silver at that. When Wagner rubbed the coin, a date appeared — 1714.

Chapter 3 ~ **SUNKEN TREASURE**

Wagner had found Spanish coins along the beach before. He'd plucked them right out of the sand, even given them away as gifts to friends. This one, though, seemed different. Not because of its shape or size or colour. Not even because of its date. Many of the coins he had found were just as old. No, this one was different because of *where* and *how* he had found it.

By the shore. After a turbulent storm.

Wagner knew that centuries ago, Spanish ships regularly sailed across the Atlantic carrying gold, silver and other priceless goods from the New World to Spain. For protection from pirates, the ships travelled together in tight packs, starting their journey in Cuba, then sailing north up the Florida coastline to catch the Gulf Stream that would help carry them across the Atlantic. The journey was dangerous and had to be perfectly timed to escape hurricanes that swirled across the ocean. Many ships never reached their destinations, and the Florida coast was a graveyard of sunken vessels and lost treasures.

Was the coin part of a long-lost treasure hidden for centuries under the water? Wagner wondered. "I looked at the sea as I rubbed the coin," he wrote later in his book *Pieces of Eight*. "I was certain now it must have been washed ashore by the storm . . . It convinced me beyond doubt that treasure lay out there. All I had to discover was what treasure, and exactly where it lay."

Then Wagner heard a story that piqued his curiosity even more. Someone told him about a flotilla of Spanish ships carrying priceless cargo that had sunk off the Florida coast in 1715. Most of the treasure had never been recovered. Wagner wondered if his coin was from the doomed fleet — and if there was more treasure out there.

With a friend's help, Wagner looked into the matter. He contacted museum officials, spoke to history experts and read stories about the 1715 fleet. Slowly, after months of careful

research, a story began to emerge — a tale of lost treasure and broken dreams unlike any he had heard before.

~

On July 24, 1715, eleven tall and handsome galleons sailed from Havana, destined for Spain. The ships rode deep in the water, their hulls filled with weighty cargo — barrels of silver coins, bags of gold pieces, fragile porcelain and fine clothing.

> **A flotilla of Spanish ships carrying priceless cargo had sunk off the Florida coast in 1715.**

Two thousand sailors manned the fleet. For the first few days, their mood was jubilant. The journey was uneventful, the sea calm, the winds steady and sure. But by July 29 the crew became edgy and nervous. The sky grew hazy. The waves, choppy one minute, became long and rolling the next. A storm was brewing.

By the next afternoon, the sky had darkened. The wind howled. The sea heaved and rolled in wild bursts. The captain ordered the ships turned to meet the storm head-on.

That night the hurricane struck with full force. The galleons rose and fell on mountainous waves, pitching high, crashing low, crushed by tonnes of cascading water. Pushed by the roaring storm, the ships veered close to hazardous reefs and dangerous shallows.

Around two in the morning, the first ship smashed into a reef. One by one, other ships followed a similar fate. Waves pounded the galleons to splinters, toppling masts, shredding sails and breaking hulls apart. Men spilled into the sea, swallowed in huge gulps by the water. A few clawed at beams and crates, desperate to find something to keep afloat. Debris fell on some, killing them on impact.

By dawn the storm was over. Littered with timber and bodies, the beach resembled a battlefield. Only one ship had escaped the fate of the others. The rest — ten ships, more than a thousand men and millions in jewels, gold medallions, precious porcelain and Spanish coins — was missing.

Survivors scrambled up and down the coast, seeking food and shelter. There was little to be had. Food, drinking water and other essentials had gone down with the ships. Many died from exhaustion, others from illness. A small party of survivors took one of the few longboats that was still in reasonable shape and headed to St. Augustine, a mission north of the site. Others banded together on the beach, safeguarding what they could.

As the story of the tragedy spread, detachments of soldiers with supplies were sent. Salvage teams arrived, too, desperate to find the missing treasure. They quickly established an encampment of tents and flimsy structures. Some men searched the water while others roamed the beach looking for anything of value.

Recovery efforts continued for almost four years before being halted. The encampment was abandoned, and Spain gave up the search. Millions in treasure had been salvaged — but less than half what the ships carried. The rest was swept away, hidden under thick layers of swirling sand.

~

One of the first things Kip Wagner did after reading the full story of the 1715 fleet was buy a used metal detector. If he was going to find the missing treasure, he had to pinpoint its location. The best way to do that, he figured, was to locate the Spanish encampment. He searched for unnatural features in the sand, for mounds or depressions that could have been made by humans.

Wagner knew that he was in for a long and difficult search. With his trusty metal detector, he unearthed hundreds of objects

A rendering of one of the ill-fated ships that was wrecked in 1715, its treasure sinking to the ocean floor.

— tin cans, bobby pins, rusty springs, metal rods and pipes. There seemed to be no end to the junk that lay buried in the sand. But evidence of the old encampment escaped him.

Then one day he spotted a large depression in the sand and, nearby, a hole containing water. His metal detector was at home, but the site looked promising. Eagerly Wagner dug into the sand. Nothing.

Disappointed, he was about to leave when he noticed his dog drinking water from the hole. That's strange, he thought. Most holes like this held salt water, something animals avoid. This must be fresh water — perhaps from the Spanish encampment?

Wagner drove home, got his metal detector and began a careful search of the site. Almost immediately the detector let out a loud screech. Within an hour, Wagner turned up a cannonball and ship's spike. His metal detector told him there were lots of other metal objects under the ground, too, and that the site was huge.

For months Wagner searched carefully, digging through the sand, screening the soil, retrieving evidence from the past — pottery, delicate porcelain, musket balls, even a pair of cutlasses, the blades half gone from rust. One lucky day he uncovered a diamond ring, its stone embedded in a band of gleaming gold and surrounded by six smaller diamonds.

One afternoon Wagner took a break from his work and went for a swim just offshore from the dig site. There, in water 3 metres deep, he spotted four or five cannons and an anchor on the bottom. A wreck site! All along he'd known the ships had to be close to the campsite, and now he had the proof.

Wagner was convinced there were other sunken wrecks from the 1715 fleet in the area, but doing an exhaustive search of the ocean could take decades. To speed things up, he leased an airplane, hired a pilot and flew over the ocean, looking for shadows and outlines of shipwrecks in the water. The plan was less successful than hoped. Hundreds of wrecks littered the Florida coastline. From the air, it was impossible to tell which ones might belong to the 1715 fleet.

Realizing that searching by himself would take forever, in 1959 Wagner formed a partnership with seven other men, each of them as keen on treasure seeking as he was. They called themselves the Real Eight Corporation. Starting in January 1960, the men spent weekends and every minute they could spare scouting the ocean in a flimsy second-hand boat they had purchased and patched up. For months they combed the ocean. Progress was slow and, more times than not, disappointing. Sharks, eels and barracudas were constant concerns. The men spent hours underwater moving stones, sifting through sand,

only to come up empty-handed. Occasionally they'd find a cannonball, copper pot or piece of pottery, but greater treasure eluded them.

By August, frustration was at a high point. Then their luck changed. One morning while searching a promising site, Harry Cannon, one of the divers, found a half-buried object the size of his fist in the sand. It was heavy, wedge-shaped and covered with encrustations. To the inexperienced eye, it looked worthless, but Cannon felt there was promise in the clump. Using a crowbar, he scraped away the crusty covering. Bright shiny metal gleamed from underneath. Silver!

The name Real Eight Corporation was a clever one. The silver coin found by Wagner was known as a piece of eight. In Spanish terms, it was worth eight *reals.*

Excited by the find, Cannon sifted through the sand and soon found five other wedge-shaped objects. Tucking them under his arm, he surfaced to show his prize to the others. Soon everyone was in the water, tossing stones aside, searching through debris. Three more wedges were pulled from the sea.

For the rest of the season, the men searched the site, harvesting what they could of the remaining treasure. Other than a few more silver wedges, the site was a disappointment. Still, there was enough to convince them they were on the right track. The 1715 fleet and its treasure existed, and they meant to find more of it.

On January 8, 1961, after a long winter, the team resumed their hunt. This time they tried another location. Almost immediately, Dan Thompson, another diver, made an important discovery: "I came upon two large, rocklike objects that for some strange reason instinctively aroused my curiosity. They were blackish-green on the sides, about a foot and a half across, and only lightly encrusted . . . Scattered on the bottom were pockets

71

of silver pieces of eight, some singly, others fused together in little clusters of two or three."

There were almost 2000 silver coins in one of the clumps. A further search of the ocean bottom brought up other coins, some loose, others in clumps. By the end of the day, they had recovered between 3500 and 4000 coins.

It was the moment Kip Wagner had been waiting for. "I lay in bed a long time before going to sleep. Glittering, tinkling coins danced around in my head for hours. My dream — my lifelong dream — was being realized. We had found treasure, and we had found it right where I knew it had to be all these years."

Months of back-breaking searching had finally paid off. This was the rich strike they all dreamed about, and the start of other strikes to come.

In all, the Real Eight team searched eight wreck sites just off Sebastian Inlet. Among their finds were thousands of silver and gold coins, handfuls of gold rings, necklaces and bracelets, as well as items such as candlesticks, cannons, anchors, swords and muskets.

Spanish *reals* like those found off the coast of Florida.

Treasure Tips

Many metals react with salt water and eventually change colour, making them difficult to recognize as treasure if they have been in the ocean for a long time:

• Silver takes on a black appearance as it reacts with salt.

• Brass and bronze turn green over time.

• Gold remains true to its original yellow appearance, and can be as shiny as the day it went down.

• Coral coats many objects, camouflaging them and changing their original shapes.

• Glass may take on a milky appearance as its surface becomes pitted, flaked and cracked when it reacts with salt water.

• Blackish clumps may be more than they seem. As silver coins and other metal objects react with salt and become covered with sea growth, they often fuse together in dark clumps, disguising their true value and making them difficult to recognize.

• Wood can deteriorate quickly. The timbers of wooden ships rot and weaken and are usually the first materials to disappear, unless they lie buried beneath protective layers of sand and silt. In some regions wood is attacked by the *teredo* or shipworm, which burrows into the wood and dissolves it.

Foul-Weather Treasures

Breezy Discovery

In 1939, in Ann Arbor, Michigan, discarded papers were discovered blowing down a street. Workers clearing a house had dumped papers into a garbage can outside, and a sudden gust of wind had carried some of them off. Fortunately, one of the wind-tossed papers fell into the hands of a knowledgeable collector. It turned out to be an envelope with one of the world's rarest stamps. The collector rushed to the trash bin and rescued as many other envelopes — and valuable stamps — as he could.

Hurricane Payoff

Big storms sometimes scrape sand off the beach and nearby dunes, exposing gold, silver and gems sunk and scattered centuries ago. In 2004, right after Hurricane Jeanne battered the Atlantic coast, marine archaeologist Joel Ruth used a metal detector to comb the Florida shoreline near the site where Kip Wagner had located the 1715 fleet. He spotted a Spanish silver coin on the beach. "I grabbed it and then every foot it was — bam, bam — another hit," he said. After four hours of searching, the batteries of his metal detector died. By then Ruth had found more than 180 silver coins worth more than $40,000.

Surprise Christmas Present

Marc Tremblay found his Christmas present underneath 3 metres of water. As he was mooring his boat on Christmas Eve 1994, Tremblay spotted some submerged objects half buried in the sand near his cottage along the St. Lawrence River. A strong storm had swept through the area, scraping away layers of sediment and revealing pots, rifles, axes, bottles and the timbers of a ship.

Archaeologists found that the wreck was the *Elizabeth and Mary*, one of thirty-two English ships that had been led in a doomed attack on Quebec City in 1690. After a hasty retreat, the ship, and three others in the fleet, sank in a wild storm. For three centuries the ship lay buried beneath the river. It took another storm and Tremblay's keen eye to bring it to the surface once again.

 South Tyrol Museum of Archaeology, Bolzano, Italy

Iceman

Two German hikers, Helmut Simon and his wife, Erika, got the surprise of their lives as they were hiking through the Alps on September 19, 1991 — they discovered a body embedded in a slowly melting glacier. Helmut took a photo of the body, then the two continued down the mountain and alerted authorities. They figured it was an unfortunate mountain climber who had slipped and fallen to his death, but what the Simons had found was a five-thousand-year-old mummy, one of the oldest and best-preserved human mummies ever discovered. Scientists believe the Iceman died from an arrow wound, then over time became covered with snow and ice. Modern climate changes had melted the glacier, bringing the long-hidden body to the surface again.

Something Terrific

When Donald Johanson awoke on the morning of November 30, 1974, he had a feeling "something terrific might happen." And it did. As Johanson, a paleoanthropologist, walked along a gully in Ethiopia, Africa, that had been created by a flash flood, he spotted a small object sticking out of the eroded bank. It was a fossilized arm bone. Nearby he found other bone fragments, all of them human-like and very old. They proved to be the remains of an adult female who lived millions of years ago. Johanson called his find Lucy, after a popular Beatles song of the day. Lucy was the oldest and most complete prehistoric human ancestor discovered up until that time.

 Man in the Galilee Museum, Nof Ginosar, Israel

Drought Yields Boat

When a severe drought struck Israel in 1985–1986, it brought an unexpected bonus. The water level in the Sea of Galilee dropped, exposing areas of the sea floor never seen before. In January 1986, two fishermen — brothers Yuval and Moshe Lufan — spotted a murky outline in the mud along the shoreline. It turned out to be a fishing boat built two thousand years ago. The mud had acted as a preservative, keeping out air and

corrosive elements that might have destroyed the wood.

The boat was constructed of twelve different kinds of wood, including sycamore, laurel, oak, and cedar from Lebanon. It was originally equipped with both sails and oars so it could be used for fishing and for transporting goods and passengers. The Galilee Boat — or the "Kinneret Boat," as the vessel has been called in Israel — matches descriptions of fishing vessels given in the Bible, and was likely the same kind of craft used to sail the sea during the time of Jesus.

Treasure Tips

Any significant object that you might discover — from a fossil to an ancient coin — might provide valuable information about the past. If possible, leave the item where it was found and alert an expert such as a museum official, palaeontologist, archivist or other knowledgeable adult to its location.

If you must pick up the object to protect it from loss or damage, wrap it carefully and remember where it was found, so that experts can examine the location.

Chapter 3 ~ **SUNKEN TREASURE**

Looted Treasure

The moment Mensun Bound spotted the broken jar, he knew it was special. Would he be able to find the rest of the treasure before it was too late?

Mensun Bound's gaze drifted across the room. His friend, a writer, was talking about sailing, but Bound was distracted, his attention suddenly drawn to a bookshelf in the corner. Pottery and books cluttered the shelves, but for Bound, one object stood out from the rest. A broken jar.

Most people wouldn't have noticed the small fragment. But twenty-eight-year-old Bound, an archaeologist, was trained to recognize fine details, and the handle caught his eye. It was elegant, curved and flowing. Most unusual. Was this really what he thought it was?

He was certain that the broken jar was Etruscan, made thousands of years ago in a region of Italy now known as Tuscany. The Etruscans had been a gifted people — artistic, musical, excellent sailors. But the Etruscans had vanished long ago. While they had left statues, jewellery and graceful homes as evidence of their past, no written records had been found, no ships recovered. Little was known about their everyday lives.

And now this Etruscan jar, on a bookshelf in his friend's London home. What a treasure!

"Where did you get this?" Bound blurted.

"That? At Giglio," his friend answered. "Twenty years ago."

Giglio is a small Tuscan island off the west coast of Italy. The writer explained that in 1961 he had vacationed on the island and gone spear fishing with a man named Reg Vallintine, who ran a diving school. On one dive they had stumbled across some ancient artifacts scattered along a steep underwater slope.

Word of their discovery spread, attracting other divers to

the site. Removing artifacts without permission from authorities was illegal, but that didn't stop souvenir hunters, who stormed the site. One by one, treasured objects vanished from the sea floor, taken by those eager for their own piece of the past. Worried that all the artifacts would disappear, Vallintine dived to the site and, after photographing some of the objects, buried the rest.

Bound listened with fascination to his friend's story. So there *were* other pieces, some still under the sea, others in the hands of looters. If he could locate them, what a find that would be. But where should he start? Reg Vallintine seemed to be the key. He had taken photographs, kept records of each dive and knew the whereabouts of the Giglio site. Bound located him in London, England, and the moment he looked at Vallintine's photos, he knew. These were Etruscan pieces, all right.

It would take more than photographs to organize a diving expedition, however. Bound needed money, divers and permission from the Italian government. To obtain these he would need to prove that the treasure actually existed. He would need real samples, actual artifacts from the sea floor.

Knowing that many artifacts had fallen into the hands of divers like his friends, Bound read Vallintine's journal, combing it for clues. There he found the first names of some divers. It wasn't much, but it was a start. With the help of Joanna Yellowlees, another archaeologist, he began a search for the looted treasure. The two scoured Europe, following a thin trail of clues. The relics were scattered in the homes of divers or their friends. In London they found an amphora, or storage jar, propping open a door. In Monte Carlo, an elegant vase in a living room.

Piece by piece they gathered the missing evidence. The artifacts were enough to convince Italian authorities to grant them permission to excavate the site. To raise money Yellowlees and Bound applied for grants and sold or pawned almost everything they owned.

Chapter 3 ~ **SUNKEN TREASURE**

On September 2, 1982, Bound, Yellowlees, Vallintine and a team of volunteer divers arrived in Giglio. It had taken a year to get to this critical point. With hopes running high, they hurried to the site pinpointed by Vallintine. Nearby, they spotted fifteen small boats and dozens of divers bobbing in the water, all searching for the same treasure. After twenty-one years, was there any treasure left to be found?

The next day Bound and Vallintine dived to the site. The sea floor seemed clean, swept clear of treasure. Then, on the fourth dive, Bound spotted several pieces of pottery jutting from the sand. Further searching uncovered other articles strewn along a steep underwater slope. At the end of the trail, in deep, dangerous waters, they located the wreck of an Etruscan ship. To

Urns like this show the traditional Estruscan features — elegant, curved, flowing lines.

Bound and Yellowlees, this was more treasure than they ever dreamed possible.

It soon became clear why looters had missed the ship and so much of its cargo. On the day of its sinking, the ship had struck a reef 200 metres offshore and must have sunk in seconds. The broken vessel would have slid down the steep slope, bouncing off rocks, scraping against coral, spilling precious cargo along the way. Finally, the keel likely plowed into the sandy bottom, and the vessel shuddered to a stop. Buried in sand below water 50 metres deep, the wreck was beyond reach of most divers. Souvenir hunters had picked the shallows clean. Few had ventured farther down the slope.

For three seasons the team dived to the site, clearing away debris, unearthing artifacts, photographing them and plotting their positions before bringing them to the surface. However, the excavation was fraught with difficulties. The ship's depth meant that divers could work at the site for only 18 minutes at a time. On their way to the surface, they had to stop in stages to allow the nitrogen absorbed by their bodies to dissolve. To rise too quickly could cause paralysis or even death.

As much as possible, they kept their work secret. Souvenir hunters lurked nearby, anxious to scoop up treasure for themselves. Under tight security, artifacts were smuggled to the surface, disguised and carried past sightseers on the beach. Yellowees even laid a false trail of underwater ropes to sidetrack would-be looters.

The ship and its cargo proved to be the find of a lifetime. In all, more than seven thousand items were salvaged. The ship dated to 600 B.C., making it the first Etruscan ship and the oldest merchant vessel ever found in the Mediterranean Sea. Each artifact brought to the surface — a leather writing tablet, an oil lamp, a delicately carved table leg — shed light on the mysterious Etruscans and their culture.

Chapter 3 ~ SUNKEN TREASURE

What was it like to be part of this discovery? Perhaps Gian Luigi Sacco, one of the divers, sums up the experience best: "No diving adventure anywhere compares with the excitement of uncovering a beautiful object that nobody has seen for twenty-six hundred years."

Treasure Tips

• Where an object originally sank is not necessarily where it will be found later. Divers must read the ocean's signs to decide where to search.

• Gravity affects objects in water just as it does objects on land. Shipwrecks and treasure tend to drift down slopes and toward the lowest points of the ocean floor.

• Underwater currents, tides and turbulent seas can change the location of objects, moving them great distances or burying them deeper in sand.

• Sinking vessels often spew debris over a wide area. Mapping the locations of objects retrieved from the ocean floor may provide clues to the whereabouts of the shipwreck itself.

Arabia *Steamboat Museum, Kansas City, Missouri*

Swallowed by Mud

The steamboat and its cargo had been lost somewhere on the muddy bottom of the Missouri River. Now, more than a century later, a trail of clues led treasure hunters to the strangest of places — a cornfield just outside a city.

Danger lurked beneath the Missouri River. Swift and unpredictable currents. Ragged rocks just below the waterline. Trees torn loose by the churning water, their thick limbs lodged deep in the mud.

On the evening of September 5, 1856, few of the 130 passengers aboard the steamboat *Arabia* were worried about these dangers. The sky was clear, the air crisp, the sun just beginning to set. The giant paddlewheels on the *Arabia*'s side churned the water, pushing the boat steadily upstream. On the upper deck, the pilot stood his post, watchful of every turn in the river. The steamer was fully loaded, its cargo safely secured in the hull.

The mud-choked Missouri was thick as soup, brown and dark. From above, the pilot did not see the huge tree trunk beneath the murky water. As the *Arabia* rounded a bend, the steamer slammed into the trunk, punching a gaping hole in the boat's wooden hull.

Water poured through the hole, drowning the cargo, flooding the boilers and snuffing out the fires that fuelled the engines. It spilled over the deck, and the boat keeled over on one side.

Panic gripped the once-calm steamer. The single lifeboat was freed. Confused men clambered aboard, paddled partway across the river, then regained their senses. Women and children first, they remembered. Back they came, loading as many as they could aboard the small craft, then ferrying them to safety on the riverbank. Back and forth they went, taking one load after another until all were saved.

The riverboat sank quickly, settling deep into the thick mud. By the next morning, only the smokestacks and the top of the pilothouse could be seen. Then these too disappeared, swept away by the current, absorbed by the sludge. Gone was the *Arabia*'s cargo — its four hundred barrels of Kentucky bourbon, its crates of clothing and china destined for stores along the way, its suitcases crammed with its passengers' personal belongings.

Over the years, the Missouri River rose and fell, changed course and shifted mud from one bank to another. The location of the *Arabia* became lost. Her story, though, stayed alive. Local residents told and retold the tale of the steamer, her cargo and the disaster that befell the ship long ago.

~

David Hawley lived in Independence, Missouri and, along with his father, Bill, and brother, Greg, worked in the heating and cooling business. One day in 1985, David visited an older customer, and while he worked the two men chatted. The customer told him of the steamboats that once rode the Missouri, the dangers they encountered along the way and the many boats that had sunk over the years.

"They're still there," the man said, "deep in the mud of the Missouri. Hundreds of doomed steamers. Heaps of lost cargo and missing treasure."

The man's words stayed with David throughout the day. When he returned to the office, he shared the stranger's story with his father and brother. Later they told the story to a friend, Jerry Mackey. Wouldn't that be something, to find a lost steamer?

Captivated by the story, David and Greg Hawley began to research the history of the Missouri and the steamboats that once paddled the unruly river. They discovered that steamboat traffic along the Missouri was at its peak in the mid-1800s. The boats carried cargo up and down the river, delivering supplies and goods from town to town. Most of the four hundred steamers that had sunk in the dangerous river were victims of "snags," fallen trees hidden below the surface, ready to puncture the hulls of passing boats.

Because the river had shifted course over the years, some of those sunken steamboats were now under farmland, Hawley discovered. Those locations seemed to hold the greatest promise of recovery, and he grew excited by the possibilities. He narrowed his research, this time to ten steamboats, all under farmland. Most were too far away, too deep or difficult to reach, and, one by one, Hawley crossed them off his list.

The *Arabia* in her heyday, before the Missouri River claimed her.

Chapter 3 ~ SUNKEN TREASURE

At the end of two years of research, one name remained. *Arabia*.

According to David Hawley's calculations, the *Arabia* was now under a farm near Parkville, a small town just thirty minutes from Independence. Hawley shared the news with his father, his brother and Jerry Mackey. The possibility of finding treasure so close to home fascinated them all.

Norman Sortor, the man who owned the farm, had heard stories of the *Arabia*. In fact there had been a number of attempts to locate the steamer on his land before. Each had met with failure, and the farmer figured this one would, too. Nevertheless he gave the men permission to try. In July 1987 David Hawley walked through Sortor's field carrying old river maps and a metal detector. Two hours into his search, he detected a clear signal almost a kilometre from the river's edge. The object was large, he noted, and deep below the surface. Could this be the *Arabia?* All the clues seemed to suggest that it was. A survey ribbon was tied to a stalk of corn in the middle of the field to mark the spot.

Over the next 16 months, equipment, supplies and funds were gathered. In November 1988 the crew returned, this time with a 100-tonne crane, pumps, generators and hundreds of metres of plastic and steel pipe. Immediately there were problems. The *Arabia* lay in an old underground river channel, 14 metres below the surface, well below the waterline. Once the men reached the 6-metre level, water began flooding the site. To fix the situation, they dug twenty wells around the site, each 20 metres deep. Water pumps were installed inside the wells, generators were fired up to operate them, and the water was led through pipes to the river.

The work was exhausting and dangerous. Knee-deep in mud, chilled to the bone, worried that they might be electrocuted or swallowed by mud, the men worked steadily through freezing

temperatures. Dreams of the once-majestic *Arabia* and her cargo kept them going. Three weeks into the dig, they uncovered the first sign they were on the right track. Beneath the mud they found a giant paddlewheel, then a few days later a small shoe caught in the spokes of a ship's wheel. A mark stamped on the bottom of the shoe indicated that it was manufactured in 1849.

The type of cargo, construction of the ship, dates, and location all matched what was known about the *Arabia*. There was no doubt now. This was the long-lost steamer, and this was the first glimpse of her cargo. The discovery marked a turning point in the dig, a shift in focus from hunting for personal treasure to preserving it for others. "We all knew why we were there," David Hawley said later.

> *This was the long-lost steamer, and this was the first glimpse of her cargo.*

On December 5, 1988, the crew hit the jackpot. They lifted a wooden shipping barrel out of the mud. Inside the barrel, snuggled deep in yellow packing straw, was a single china bowl, as elegant as the day it had been tucked away for its long journey down the muddy Missouri. Below the bowl they found other items — silk, figurines, perfume bottles — 178 artifacts in all.

From that day on, there was one surprise after another: crates of unbroken dishes; cartons of food, medicine and clothing; barrels filled with guns, pocket knives, buttons and beads; hundreds of household items.

"It was like an 1856 Wal-Mart," David Hawley said later. "The boat almost became this portal into the past where you could go back to Abraham Lincoln's time and gather up an armful of stuff and bring it back into today's world and see it and smell it and taste it."

For four months the work continued day and night. Parts of the steamer were located. The 11-tonne boiler, sections of the

The huge paddlewheel from the *Arabia.*

paddlewheel, the steam engine, a portion of the stern — these were all hoisted out of the site by the crane. The team consulted an archaeologist to ensure that each item was carefully documented and removed. In all, two hundred thousand objects were recovered, making the *Arabia* the single greatest find of pre–American-Civil-War artifacts.

On Saturday evening, February 11, 1989, the work ended. Spring was approaching, and Norman Sortor needed the field for farming. The pumps were turned off, the cranes and bulldozers removed. Within hours, the pit filled with water, covering what little remained of the *Arabia.*

The artifacts were worth millions of dollars, but rather than sell the items, the partners decided to open a museum and share the find with others. By charging admission, they could recover their costs, which by then totalled more than $750,000. First, though, each item had to be catalogued, cleaned and preserved — once out of their protective layer of mud and in the open air, the items would disintegrate easily. Huge coolers were used to freeze and stabilize the more fragile artifacts. Cool caves and large vats of water kept other items intact. Specialists were hired to conserve and restore delicate objects.

The *Arabia* Steamboat Museum opened in Kansas City, Missouri, on November 13, 1991, almost three years after excavations had begun. Only a small portion of the immense collection of items was put on display, and since that time preservation, documentation and study of the *Arabia* and its cargo have continued.

Meanwhile, the Hawleys are on to other pursuits. Dozens of steamboats, each with its own story to tell, lie deep in the mud along the Missouri, and the treasure seekers have their sights set on adding others to their collection.

Is There Treasure in Your Backyard?

Backyard Cache

When he was growing up, Mark Biederman, an Ontario veterinarian, heard stories about his family's long-lost treasure. During World War II, the Nazis had deported his father, Harry Biederman, and other family members from their homes in Lodz, Poland. Because they were allowed to take along only a small amount of money each, the family coin collection was hastily stuffed into a ceramic pot and buried in the backyard for safekeeping.

But the Biederman family became displaced by the war — victims of the Holocaust. Five of Mark Biederman's immediate family lost their lives. Others survived and moved to Canada and the United States. The ceramic pot, with its 63 gold coins, some dating to 1703, remained hidden and largely forgotten for more than sixty years. Then Mark recalled the stories and, after a decade-long search, tracked down the missing treasure stash. In April 2004 the pot and its coins were located, still buried in the backyard of what had been the family home in Lodz.

 Regional Historical Museum, Vratsa, Bulgaria

Some Ditch!

In the summer of 1985, Ivan Dimitrov was digging a ditch in the backyard of his home in Rogozen, Bulgaria, when his shovel clinked against something metallic. The object he pulled from the dirt looked cheap and worthless — a battered metal plate. Dimitrov tossed it aside and continued digging. To his surprise, he found other items hidden below — bowls, jugs, cups and still more plates. In a short time, Dimitrov had pulled 65 objects from the shallow pit.

Archaeologists called to the site uncovered a second cache larger than the first. It contained, among other things, 108 *phialae*, or shallow drinking cups. The archaeologists believe a noble family stashed the items during a time of turmoil twenty-five hundred years ago. The Bulgarian government reimbursed Dimitrov for his find and today his discovery — the Rogozen Treasure — is on display in Vratsa, Bulgaria.

 Somerset County Museum, Somerset, England

Beginner's Luck

A few minutes after being shown how to use a metal detector, thirty-three-year-old Kevin Elliott struck it rich. In August 1998 he discovered a Roman silver coin buried beneath a gateway at his family's farm in Shapwick, Somerset, England. With his cousin Martin he searched further and uncovered a scattering of coins. Eagerly, the pair scooped them into milk buckets. Thirty minutes later, the two men struck the motherlode — a huge hoard of thousands of silver coins dating from 31 B.C. to 224 A.D. "The odds of finding something like this in such a short space of time are phenomenal, mind-boggling," said Martin.

Archaeologists believe the Shapwick Coin Hoard, a stash of over nine thousand coins, had been buried beneath the floor of an ancient courtyard villa that once stood upon the site. The Somerset County Museum purchased the treasure from the two cousins for £265,000.

 The British Museum, London, England

Burial Boat

In 1939 archaeologists probed earth mounds found on the property of Mrs. Edith Pretty, near the estate of Sutton Hoo in Suffolk, England. Deep beneath the soil, they discovered an immense burial site. Under one of the largest mounds, they uncovered the remains of a boat over 8 metres long. In the centre of the boat, where there had once been a chamber, they found amazing treasures — heavy gold jewellery, gem-encrusted swords and sceptres, silver bowls, dishes and spoons, and a gold purse containing twenty-seven gold coins. No body was found, but the richness of treasure indicated that it was a royal burial site, perhaps of a powerful king named Raedwald who died around 624 A.D. Today the Sutton Hoo Treasure is on display in the British Museum in London.

 Keltenmuseum Hochdorf, Hochdorf, Germany

No Stone Unturned

When farmers in Hochdorf, Germany, complained about the large number of stones beneath a huge mound of dirt in their fields, Jorg Biel's thoughts turned to treasure. The farmers were frustrated by the stones that lay beneath the soil, damaging their plows and slowing their progress. But Biel, an archaeologist, figured the stones might actually be part of something else — a huge stone tomb buried beneath the mound. In the late 1970s he excavated the site and uncovered the bones and golden possessions of a Celtic noble who had lived twenty-five hundred years ago. The body was decorated with jewels, wore silk-embroidered clothes and gold-laced shoes, and was accompanied by dozens of other precious objects.

Ramses Rises Again

In 2006 archeologists discovered several statues under a busy outdoor marketplace in Cairo, Egypt. One was a 2-metre-tall statue of a seated figure bearing hieroglyphics that included three references to Ramses II, a king who ruled Egypt during the thirteenth century B.C. Also found was a 4- to 5-tonne pink granite statue with features resembling those of the Egyptian king. Archeologists believe they have located an ancient sun temple which, over time, became buried under more modern structures as the city grew.

The Catch of a Lifetime

The expensive net was ripped. As the trawler's winch was hauled from the sea, the catch spilled into the water. Suddenly one of the men cried, "Coins! Coins!"

August 2, 1993, was a discouraging day for the crew of the fishing trawler, *The Mistake*. In water 91 metres deep, 80 kilometres south of Louisiana on the choppy Gulf of Mexico, the ship's net snagged and caught on something — an overhang, maybe. Or an outcropping of rock, perhaps. The winch growled and complained as it tugged, straining to loosen the net. When the net finally snapped free and the winch returned to its familiar purring, relief spread among the crew.

It was short-lived. The expensive net was torn, and as it surfaced, its contents spilled into the water like the insides of a gutted fish. The net would have to be repaired — another setback to an already sour day. And the contents? Not fish at all, but chunks of rocks. Hundreds of them. Worthless and trickling out of the net into the sea.

The gutted net was hauled out of the water and the crew readied itself to dump the remaining debris overboard. Suddenly one of the men cried, "Coins! Coins!"

Jerry Murphy, the captain of *The Mistake*, rushed to take a closer look. There, dropping from the net like water drops from a leaking bucket, were hundreds of coins. Silver. Spanish. All, they soon realized, stamped with the same date — 1783.

This was the catch of a lifetime. While the men whooped and hollered, Jerry Murphy calmed himself and tried to make sense of the prize. The net must have snagged on a Spanish shipwreck — a very old one, judging from the date on the coins. Quietly, Murphy recorded the location on his plotter.

The trip back to the dock was a long one. Murphy turned

the coins over in his hand in wonder. There had to be more of them hidden under the water. Back on shore, Murphy placed a call to Jim Reahard, his uncle and part-owner of *The Mistake*.

"Well, boss, I've got good news and bad news," Murphy began. "The bad news is that I just tore up your net. The good news is that I just made the best catch of my life."

There were wild celebrations that night. Jim Reahard and his wife, Myra, laughed, giggled, and danced a jig around their kitchen table. Jerry Murphy dreamed of mountains of treasure below the watery sea.

> *Only one ship matched the clues. It was* El Cazador *— The Hunter.*

Before long, though, reality hit home. What treasure was this? they wondered. What would they need to do to claim it?

The Reahards contacted a lawyer, David Paul Hornan, who specialized in deep-sea salvage. He would know how to file a salvage claim and how to protect their rights. Then they hired Robert Stenuit, a researcher and expert in maritime history. He might be able to tell them what ship they had found.

Stenuit went to the Archive of the Indies in Seville, Spain. The Spanish had kept careful records of each ship and its cargo and he was hopeful he could track one down that had sunk in this location. As well as being dated 1783, the coins were stamped with the image of a king and marked *Carolus III*.

Only one ship matched the clues.

El Cazador — The Hunter.

El Cazador was a two-masted, square-rigged wooden vessel, one of many ships in the Spanish fleet. According to the records, on January 11, 1784, at a time when Carolus III was king of Spain, *El Cazador* left Vera Cruz, Mexico, and sailed for New Orleans, Louisiana, on the other side of the Gulf of Mexico. The ship carried the king's treasure — four hundred and fifty thousand gold and silver coins.

A gold coin such as those found at the *El Cazador* wreck site.

The coins were desperately needed in Spanish Louisiana, where Spanish paper money was commonly used as currency. But paper money was easy to counterfeit, and the Louisiana territory had become flooded with phony, useless bills. The value of the bills had plummeted, putting the entire economy at risk. The Spanish government was on the verge of collapse. Something had to be done and quickly, too.

King Carolus III saw only one way out: replace the paper money with coins — which were almost impossible to counterfeit — thereby shoring up the economy and bringing stability to the Spanish colony once again. He ordered his vast coin reserve transferred from Mexico to New Orleans, then waited, hoping that his plan would work.

El Cazador never did arrive in New Orleans. A search was organized. The waters were combed, the coastline inspected.

There was no sign of the ship, no word of survivors, no trace of the treasure.

The results were catastrophic. Without the coins, the Louisiana economy floundered and stalled. In 1800 Spanish Louisiana was lost to France. Three years later it was sold to the United States, instantly doubling the size of the fledgling country.

El Cazador was never heard of again. Not until August 2, 1993, that is, when *The Mistake*'s net scraped against the sunken vessel, catching a heap of the glittering prize and bringing it to the surface for the first time in over two hundred years.

Convinced that they had correctly identified the ship, the Reahards, Jerry Murphy and a few others formed a partnership. They filed a salvage claim and began the process of retrieving the treasure.

This was no easy task. The ship was submerged in deep water, making it hard to reach. Divers had to wear specially designed diving suits, and a one-man submersible was employed to help with the search. Many of the coins were in clumps and needed to be separated and cleaned. Costs soared.

> *There was no sign of the ship, no word of survivors, no trace of the treasure.*

In spite of the difficulties and expense, the partnership has been successful. More than three hundred thousand coins have been retrieved, their total value more than $1 million. The discovery of *El Cazador* has been, in Jim Reahard's words, "an experience that most people never even dream of in their lifetime."

Lost & Found
Sunken Treasure

National Archeological Museum, Athens, Greece

Found: The Antikythera Wreck

In October 1900 Greek sponge diver Elias Stadiatis rushed back to the surface minutes after plunging into the Mediterranean Sea near the island of Antikythera. "Horses! Women!" he sputtered in terror. Stadiatis claimed to have seen a whole city of dead animals and people on the sea floor. The captain dove into the water to check for himself, tied a rope to an object below, and ordered the crew to haul it aboard. It was a bronze hand, the first evidence of great treasure. The find turned out to be an ancient Roman ship and its cargo of bronze statues. Although divers sold some of the smaller statues before officials were notified, many of the surviving pieces of the Antikythera treasure were collected by authorities and can be seen on display at the National Archeological Museum in Athens, Greece.

Lost: The *Admiral Nakhimov* Treasure

In 1905, at the height of the two-year Russian–Japanese War, the Russian battle ship *Admiral Nakhimov* was struck by torpedoes as it entered the Tsushima Strait between Korea and Japan. The crew was rescued, but to keep the wounded ship out of Japanese hands, the captain scuttled the vessel, sending

the ship to the bottom near the Japanese island of Tsushima. "I sank the things which I was bringing you in fifty fathoms of sea, and they can never be utilized by the enemy," the captain wrote to the czar. Some say a vast treasure of more than five thousand boxes of gold coins and ingots was aboard.

Found: The *Central America*

Since the steamship *Central America* sank in a hurricane off the coast of South Carolina on September 12, 1857, dozens of treasure seekers have dreamed of finding the lost vessel. The wooden sidewheeler was returning to New York carrying 578 passengers, many of them miners and millionaires fresh from the gold fields of California. In its hold, the ship carried 3 tons of gold and hundreds of rare coins. Four hundred and twenty-five passengers and crew died in the disaster, and the loss of the *Central America*'s vast treasure set off an economic depression across the United States.

For over a century the wreck could not be found. Enter Tommy Thompson, an Ohio engineer. Using computers, sonar and remote-controlled, deep-diving robotic submersibles, Thompson and his crew located the wreck in 1986 after only forty days of searching, and retrieved its cargo of gold bars and coins. Thompson said, "I never dreamed it would be like this. It's just like a storybook treasure." The *Central America*'s cargo may be worth as much as $1 billion, making it one of the most commercially successful salvages of all time.

Lost: The *Santa Maria*

Three ships accompanied Christopher Columbus on his voyage to the New World. The largest of these was the lead ship, the *Santa Maria*. On Christmas Eve, 1492, the *Santa Maria* struck

a Caribbean reef and became wedged tight, unable to move. Columbus was forced to abandon the ship and leave thirty-nine sailors behind on the island of Haiti. He instructed the men to build a fort with planks from the *Santa Maria*. When he returned the following year, Columbus found the burned remains of the fort and not one of the sailors alive.

More than five centuries later, the search for the world's most historic ship is in full swing. Archaeologists think they have found the site of the fort in northern Haiti. They believe that the *Santa Maria* cannot lie far offshore. After five centuries in the salty water, likely all that remains of the vessel is the rocks it carried as ballast. To historians, that would be treasure enough. The rocks, if found, could be traced to sources in Europe, providing scholars with new information about the *Santa Maria*'s origin and construction.

 Mel Fisher's Museum, Key West, Florida

Found: The *Atocha*

For diver Mel Fisher, finding *La Nuestra Señora de Atocha* became an obsession. In 1969 Fisher began a quest to find the sunken Spanish galleon and its immense treasure. At first Fisher searched the head of the Florida Keys for the phantom wreck. Years later he discovered that he was looking in the wrong spot. Careful research of Spanish records revealed that the *Atocha* had gone down about 32 kilometres away. Fisher relocated his dive team and kept their spirits alive with promises of bountiful treasure. "Just wait until you see the main pile," he told them at one point. "There'll be stacks of silver bars lined up like a brick wall on the ocean floor. There'll be bars of gold and treasure chests filled with gold and silver coins. It's all there. Believe me."

On July 13, 1975, divers discovered brass cannons and hundreds of silver coins, the first signs that Fisher was finally on the *Atocha*'s trail. On July 20, 1985, divers hit the jackpot, locating not only the wreck of the *Atocha*, but a treasure worth US$400 million at the time — chests of silver coins and solid gold bars, more than nine hundred silver ingots, each weighing 32 kilograms, and an assortment of priceless items ranging from heavy gold chains to solid gold plates.

Found: *Le Chameau* and the *Feversham*

In 1965, after five years of searching, Alex Storm discovered the wreck of *Le Chameau*, a French sailing vessel that sank off the coast of Cape Breton, Nova Scotia, during a violent storm in 1725. By following the trail of debris, Storm and his crew were able to recover much of *Le Chameau*'s rich cargo — thousands of gold and silver coins as well as silver forks, buckles, sword hilts, and even a gold ring with a large emerald.

In 1968 Storm and his diving partners found a second vessel in Cape Breton's waters — the *Feversham*, a treasure-rich English ship that sank during a storm in 1711. Since then, other shipwrecks have been found off the coast of Cape Breton, among them *L'Africaine*, a French ship loaded with gold and silver bullion, and *Le Triton*, a Spanish ship carrying riches bound for Spain.

Still Missing: The *Fantome*

There's more treasure to be found, too. Over the past four centuries, an estimated ten thousand sailing vessels have met untimely ends in Cape Breton's treacherous waters, making the region one of the richest, and most lucrative, shipwreck graveyards in the world. One of the most historically valuable wrecks awaiting discovery is the *Fantome*, a British naval vessel that ran aground on a dangerous shoal south of Halifax in November 1814. Fresh from attacks on Washington in the War of 1812, the *Fantome* reputedly was carrying loot stolen from the White House and Capitol building at the time of its sinking.

Chapter 4
BURIED TREASURE

In Their Own Words

"As my eyes grew accustomed to the light, details of the room emerged slowly from the mist: strange animals, statues, and gold — everywhere the glint of gold."
Howard Carter, describing his discovery of King Tutankhamen's tomb

"It's spooky down there, it's dangerous, it's chancy."
Pat Epps, on the risks taken to find the Lost Squadron

"We understood suddenly that the people we'd seen in drawings — and their ceremonies, their rituals — were real."
Walter Alva, on the importance of the royal tombs found in Sipan, Peru

"They bound his coffins, the first with gold, the second with silver, the third with the strength of iron, showing by such device that these suited a most mighty king."
A witness describing the elaborate burial of Attila the Hun

Chapter 4 ~ **BURIED TREASURE**

Secrets of Boscoreale

Beneath the trap door, sprawled on the floor, was a body, and around it the glittering gold of treasure in the flickering light.

Death came quickly. It caught the man by surprise, snuffing out his life so suddenly that the treasure in his hands hit the floor before his body did. Bracelets, earrings, chains and hundreds of gold coins tumbled across the marble tile, rolling in all directions, clattering noisily.

The man heard none of this. The volcano's roar was the last sound to fill his ears. That was just seconds before a wave of ash covered the trap door, swallowed the villa and smothered the entire town.

Under the mountain of ash, the man and his treasure remained hidden for centuries. Then Vincenzo de Prisco discovered the secret and, by unlocking it, created another of his own.

~

Signor Vincenzo de Prisco was late that Easter Sunday in 1895. Sunday was payday and the workmen who had been digging on de Prisco's land were eager for their boss to show up. After working hard all week, they wanted their wages. Where was Signor de Prisco? It wasn't like him to be so late.

De Prisco's property was in Boscoreale, a tiny town perched near the top of Mount Vesuvius in central Italy. Although the town itself was centuries old, what lay beneath it was even older. In 79 A.D., Vesuvius had erupted, spewing ash down the mountain, engulfing entire towns, killing residents, stopping them cold in their tracks. Beneath the winding streets and stone buildings of Boscoreale lurked the ancient past — a Roman town frozen in time, preserved by the ash of Vesuvius.

Underneath his property, de Prisco had discovered a Roman villa almost two thousand years old, and he had hired workmen to excavate it. The villa was surprisingly intact, and each shovelful of dirt brought new surprises — graceful stone walls, statues and delicate carvings, bronze bathtubs and elegant furniture. The most spectacular find was in the main bedroom. The mistress of the house had died upon the bronze-framed bed. That was where her skeleton was found, still covered with precious jewels. In a nearby corridor lay a slave, a few coins clutched tightly in his bony hands.

But now it was Sunday, payday, and Signor de Prisco was nowhere to be seen. The workmen grew restless. Why not keep digging? one suggested. He pointed to a small opening in the floor that led to the family wine cellar. Surely Signor de Prisco won't mind if we dig there.

Around the skeleton, the glitter of gold in the flickering light . . .

Originally a wooden trap door had covered the opening. Now there was only a hole in the floor. It was plugged with ash, but once that was cleared, the men saw that it led to a larger space below. They selected a man named Michele to squeeze through the narrow opening to see what he could find.

Inside, the light was dim. As Michele's eyes adjusted to the darkness, he spotted shadowy forms. A man was sprawled on the floor, skeletal hands clasped together as if holding a precious prize. Around the skeleton, the glitter of gold in the flickering light . . . chains, earrings, bracelets and hundreds of coins strewn across the floor. Then, beyond the skeleton, at the cellar's far end, other treasures — goblets, basins, cups, dishes — all black and tarnished, but clearly made of silver.

Chapter 4 ~ BURIED TREASURE

The skeleton, the coins, the scattered treasure — all told a story, and Michele was quick to piece it together. With Vesuvius shuddering and about to explode, the man must have scooped up his most precious belongings and headed to the wine cellar. He had closed the trap door, somehow thinking it would protect him. It didn't. A cloud of poisonous gas engulfed the villa, seeped into the cellar and extinguished the man's life before he could stash the coins and jewels. He fell to the floor, treasure scattering everywhere. Then a wave of ash rolled over the villa, covering the trap door and hiding the man, keeping his treasure and final act a secret for centuries.

What should I do now? Michele wondered. If he announced his discovery to the other workmen, they would scramble into the cellar, helping themselves to the treasure. No, Michele decided, it would be better to keep this a secret from them and tell only Signor de Prisco. Signor de Prisco would know what to do.

Michele stumbled back to the opening. Pretending to gasp and gag, he declared that the air was stale and conditions too dangerous to go any farther. Believing his story, the workmen abandoned the search.

That night Michele returned with Signor de Prisco. By the light of their lamps, the treasure gleamed as never before. Clearly this was an amazing find. The cellar held the entire wealth of a well-to-do Roman family.

The two men struck a bargain. Signor de Prisco would keep the treasure. After all, it had been found on his property. In return for his silence, Michele would receive a handsome reward, his to use as he pleased.

Within days Signor de Prisco had sold the treasure to a dealer, paid Michele a portion of the profits and pocketed the rest. He was confident that his secret was safe and no one would be the wiser. After all, Michele was the only one who

Skeletons surround a silver container, known as a *clotho*, unearthed from the Boscoreale site.

knew, and the man had been rewarded and sworn to silence.

But Michele went on a drinking spree with his newfound riches. The liquor loosened his tongue, and Michele boasted of his discovery. The treasure . . . you should have seen it, Michele told anyone who would listen. Heaps of gold and silver. Mountains of it now.

Word reached the Italian government. By law the treasure rightfully belonged to all Italians, not just Signor de Prisco — it was part of Italy's history and heritage. But already it was too late. The dealer had smuggled the treasure out of the country and sold all of it in Paris.

*Chapter 4 ~ **BURIED TREASURE***

Much of the Boscoreale treasure disappeared into private collections around the world. Fortunately, though, forty-one pieces were recovered and sold to the Louvre, the national museum in Paris. That's where you can see them today, restored to their original glittering state.

Museo Tumbas Reales de Sipan, Lambayeque, Peru

The Lords of Sipan

The race was on. Plucked from the hands of looters, the package held a golden mask and the promise of even greater treasure in the tombs of Sipan. Who would be the first to claim it?

Walter Alva had received calls from the police before, but the one he received on February 25, 1987, was different. It came after midnight and jarred him out of a much-needed sleep. The voice at the other end sounded urgent, too, as if on to something important.

"Can you come to the police station?" the caller asked Alva. "We have something we'd like you to see."

It was the Peruvian police. Grave robbers had been busy again, they explained. Looters had broken into a burial mound outside the town of Sipan in northern Peru, stealing offerings and artifacts that had been sealed inside. A few of the robbers had been caught red-handed, and police had confiscated their loot. Would Alva lend a hand? Would he help to identify the objects?

Walter Alva was the director of the National Bruning Museum in Lambayeque, a nearby town. He was an expert on Peru's ancient cultures, in particular the Moche, a group of people who once lived along Peru's northern coast between 100 and 800 A.D.

The Moche had been skilled farmers, fishermen, engineers and artists. They had constructed a complicated system of canals to bring water into the desert. They had also built mud-brick tombs and filled them with beautiful pottery and elegant jewellery to honour their dead.

Despite these achievements, little was known about the Moche people and their way of life. Grave robbers often discovered tombs before archaeologists did. After rifling through the treasure inside, carelessly tossing aside items considered worthless, the looters took those that could be sold quickly and easily. In their hurry to ransack the tombs they erased valuable evidence of the Moche's past.

What did police find this time? Alva wondered. Shards of pottery? Metal tools? Amulets? He had been sick with bronchitis for three days and was reluctant to leave his warm bed. But the caller was insistent, so Alva hesitantly agreed to go.

At the police station, Alva was handed a package. Inside he found a human mask made of hammered gold. The eyes were silver, the pupils made of rare cobalt-blue stones. Then the police showed Alva a dozen other things, all Moche in origin, all finer than anything Alva had seen before. Weeks before, they told him, tombs near the village of Sipan had been plundered and looted. These objects had been confiscated during police raids on the homes of suspected looters.

Can you show me the tomb where these objects came from? Alva wanted to know. He was led to a pyramid-shaped mound near Sipan. Looters were still there, scrambling over the mound, digging through the burial chamber, stripping it of treasure and carelessly ransacking its interior. Since the original break-in, many of the tomb's precious objects had been sold to eager buyers and were already in the hands of collectors around the globe.

Chapter 4 ~ **BURIED TREASURE**

Alva, a small team of colleagues and a few police officers chased away the looters. They sealed the tomb and posted an armed guard to keep away others who had rushed to the site. Then Alva and his team cleaned out the tomb and carefully examined its contents. They hoped to recover what little the looters had missed.

The tomb was constructed of mud bricks stacked in a pyramid-like shape. In one corner archaeologists noticed that the bricks had been removed. The ground seemed disturbed, as if freshly dug. Curious, they excavated the site. To their surprise it led to a second chamber, one that had been missed by the looters.

As they dug farther, the archaeologists encountered the skeleton of a man. His feet were missing. Had they been cut off to prevent him from leaving his post? they wondered. The skeleton appeared to be guarding something, but what?

> *As they dug farther, the archaeologists encountered the skeleton of a man.*

The answer was below. Beneath the skeleton was a wooden coffin and inside it the skeleton of another man surrounded by fabulous treasures — gold and silver jewellery, embroidered clothes and huge gold and feathered headdresses. The remains were poorly preserved, but appeared to belong to a man around forty years old at the time of his death. Around this coffin were five others. They contained the skeletons of two men and three women.

Clearly the gold-covered man in the main coffin was an important person, a leader or royal figure. Alva and his team called him the Lord of Sipan, after the small village nearby.

But there was still another surprise — a second tomb. Like the first, it held a wooden coffin containing the skeleton of a man surrounded by treasures. Other coffins circled this one, too, also containing skeletons of men and women. The archaeologists referred to this as Tomb 2 and the figure in the coffin as the Old Lord of Sipan.

In all, the tombs of thirteen individuals were found at Sipan. The treasure in the tombs was rich in information, providing archaeologists with a glimpse into the Moche's past never seen before. According to Alva, "This discovery revolutionized Moche studies the way the discovery of King Tut changed Egyptian studies. We understood suddenly that the people we'd seen in drawings — and their ceremonies, their rituals — were real."

A tomb of one of the royal lords of the ancient Moche culture.

The treasures of the Lords of Sipan can be seen in the Museo Tumbas Reales de Sipan, a red-coloured, pyramid-shaped museum in Lambayeque. Visitors enter the building through the top of the pyramid and wind their way down through a series of galleries in much the same way archaeologists did in the original tomb.

On their journey visitors see the bracelets that adorned the lord's wrists, the gold sheets that rested on his eyes, the gold-and-silver sceptre that had once been in his hands. Finally visitors come face to face with the skeleton of the Lord of Sipan himself. His remains and those of two other entombed figures are on display in the last exhibit, surrounded by treasure and ready for their final journey, into eternity.

 Egyptian Museum, Cairo, Egypt

Everywhere the Glint of Gold

"At last have made wonderful discovery in valley; a magnificent tomb with seals intact."

For many long years, British archaeologist Howard Carter toiled in Egypt's hot sun, digging in the dirt, chipping at brittle stones, searching — always searching — for clues to an elusive puzzle three thousand years old or more. Somewhere beneath the shifting sands of the Valley of Kings on the western bank of the Nile River lay a treasure beyond all imagination — the tomb of Tutankhamen, the boy king. And Howard Carter meant to find it.

Little was known about Tutankhamen. Ancient Egyptian documents gave sparse details about his life. Tutankhamen had assumed the throne when he was just a boy, then died mysteriously around 1350 B.C. at the age of about eighteen. In the tradition of pharaohs before him, Tutankhamen's body had been mummified and buried in a tomb in the Valley of Kings, surrounded by hundreds of golden objects, his to use in the afterlife.

Somewhere beneath the shifting sands of the Valley of Kings lay a treasure beyond all imagination.

Over time the location of the tomb was forgotten. Then, early in the 1900s, American archaeologist Theodore Davis found a cup and fragments of gold foil bearing the boy king's name. Convinced that the objects pointed the way to the tomb, Howard Carter approached his friend Lord Carnarvon to finance an expedition. With Carnarvon's support, Carter headed to the Valley of the Kings, armed with supplies and a crew of workers.

But six years of searching produced little more than frustration and disappointment. Carter's future looked bleak. Other than heaps of rubble, he had little to show for his efforts. Tutankhamen's tomb — if there even was one — was still lost in the bone-dry desert.

In 1922 Carter received devastating news. Lord Carnarvon announced that at the end of the season he would no longer support the project. It was simply too expensive to continue.

Time was running out, and so, it seemed, were Carter's chances of finding the missing tomb. Then on the morning of November 4, 1922, Carter's luck changed. He ordered his Egyptian workers to remove an ancient hut that stood on the dig site. Beneath the hut, the workers discovered a step. That led to others — twelve steps in all. The steps led to a doorway beneath the ground. At the bottom was a sealed door.

Carter broke a small hole in the door and shone a light inside. The corridor behind was filled with boulders. Carter's

Chapter 4 ~ **BURIED TREASURE**

hopes rose. Egyptian priests often filled passageways to tombs with boulders in order to discourage looters. Could this be Tutankhamen's tomb? Was there treasure inside?

Carter dared go no further. He fired off a telegram to Carnarvon: "At last have made wonderful discovery in valley; a magnificent tomb with seals intact; re-covered same for your arrival; congratulations."

Carter waited an agonizing time — almost three weeks — for Carnarvon to arrive. With his benefactor by his side, Carter made a hole in the second sealed door, thrust a candle inside, and peered into the tomb.

"At first I could see nothing," he wrote later, "the hot air escaping from the chamber causing the candle flame to flicker, but presently, as my eyes grew accustomed to the light, details of the room emerged slowly from the mist: strange animals, statues, and gold — everywhere the glint of gold." Carter stared

Carter brushes dust off the face on the coffin of King Tutankhamen.

into the room, speechless for a long while.

"Can you see anything?" Lord Carnarvon finally asked.

"Yes," Carter whispered, "wonderful things."

The room was filled floor to ceiling with hundreds of beautiful objects: chariots overlaid with gold, elegant couches and gold-lined chairs, life-size statues clothed in jewels and gold, and dozens of toys, ornaments, vases, dishes and other vessels. But the room was just the beginning of wondrous surprises. Beyond it, Carter found another room also packed with golden treasures, and deeper into the tomb a burial chamber containing a series of coffins, one inside the other. In the innermost coffin, made entirely of gold, he found the most valuable treasure of all — the mummified body of the young pharaoh, Tutankhamen.

It was a stunning end to Carter's seven-year search. He had found the missing tomb and its spectacular treasure. In doing so, he gave the world another treasure. He opened the door to a largely unknown period of Egyptian history. Today many of the objects Carter unearthed are on display in the Egyptian Museum in Cairo, a reminder of Egypt's glorious past, a tribute to the archaeologist who uncovered it.

~

For a time, archeologists believed that Tutankhamen's tomb would be the last one found in the Valley of Kings. Since then, however, others have been located. In 2006 archeologists announced the discovery of a new tomb near Tutankhamen's. Like the boy king's, the new tomb was located beneath the remains of ancient workmen's huts, at the bottom of a narrow shaft leading to a door made of stone. The new tomb, dubbed KV63, contained five wooden sarcophagi surrounded by alabaster jars. Although KV63 is probably not a royal tomb, the discovery opens the possibility that other tombs may still be hidden in the Valley of Kings.

Other Lost & Found Royal Tombs

Beijing Palace Museum, Beijing, China

Found: Tombs of Prince Liu Sheng and Princess Dou Wan

In 1968 Chinese soldiers stumbled upon a small hole in the rocky hillside near the town of Mancheng, 150 kilometres southwest of Beijing. The hole led to an enormous underground chamber that was the burial site of Prince Liu Sheng, a ruler who died in 113 B.C. On a nearby hill, soldiers found a second tomb, that of Princess Dou Wan, Liu Sheng's wife.

The tombs were filled with thousands of objects, including swords, bowls and hundreds of pots and statuettes laid out in rows on the chamber floors. In two side passages of Liu Sheng's tomb, archaeologists found six carriages and the skeletons of sixteen horses and eleven dogs. The most dazzling discoveries, however, were the prince and princess's burial suits. Although the bodies had rotted away, the burial suits had survived, each made of thousands of small squares of polished jade linked together by gold wire.

Qin Shi Huang Mausoleum, Xian, China

Found: The Tomb of Shi Huang Ti

In 1974 peasants from the town of Xian, China, were digging a well along the valley of the Yellow River when they struck something hard. Thinking the obstacle was a stone, they struggled to remove it. The "hard stone" turned out to be a terracotta soldier, a life-size figure made of baked clay.

Further excavation revealed other wonders. The soldier was the first of almost eight thousand terracotta figures buried in three chambers underground. Each soldier bore different facial features and carried weapons such as swords, crossbows, javelins, and bows and arrows. Actual-size terracotta horses pulling chariots were also uncovered. The soldiers and horses stand guard outside the tomb of Shi Huang Ti, the first emperor of a unified China and the builder of the Great Wall of China more than two thousand years ago.

Lost: The Tomb of Attila the Hun

Possible location: *Near Budapest, Hungary*

Attila the Hun and his armies battled the Roman Empire for twenty years, weakening it and causing it to crumble. In 453 A.D., when the powerful leader was about forty-seven, he married a beautiful Germanic girl. On the wedding night, Attila reportedly suffered a severe nosebleed, choked and suffocated.

His funeral was a major event. According to a witness, "They bound his coffins, the first with gold, the second with silver, the third with the strength of iron, showing by such device that these suited a most mighty king." Precious stones, gold and silver ornaments, and weapons were deposited in the grave. To keep its location a secret, slaves who dug the grave were slaughtered and buried as well.

Lost: The Tomb of Alexander the Great

Possible location: *Alexandria, Egypt*

Alexander the Great was only thirty-two years old when he died of suspicious causes in 323 B.C., but he had already conquered vast territories and made a name for himself as the wealthy ruler of a huge empire. According to ancient accounts, his funeral was a lavish affair. His body was placed in a gold sarcophagus shaped like a man. The sarcophagus was placed inside a second gold casket, then carried atop a wagon from Babylon to Alexandria, Egypt. There it was entombed along with weapons, cups, plates and fine jewellery fashioned from silver and gold.

For decades afterwards his grave was visited and honoured by emperors and kings. Legend has it that Alexander's golden sarcophagus was later stolen, switched with a glass one, and melted to fashion coins for his successor. The whereabouts of Alexander's grave and the original sarcophagus are unknown.

Lost: **The Tomb of Alaric**

Possible location: *Near Cosenza, Italy*

Alaric was a young king of the Visigoths, who died in 410 A.D. Alaric's burial is even more memorable than any of his known achievements. According to legend, Alaric's followers chose a most unusual burial site to foil grave robbers — the bottom of the Busento River. First, prisoners were forced to build a dike to divert the river. Then, along the exposed riverbed, they dug a huge trench. After Alaric and his belongings were buried in the trench, the dike was destroyed, the river was returned to its normal course, and the prisoners were killed to keep the secret. Rumour has it that 25 tonnes of gold and 150 tonnes of silver lie buried with Alaric.

Lost City in the Sand

The road wound through the desert, disappearing for long stretches, then reappearing as if by magic. Was this the legendary road to Ubar, the majestic lost city? Nicholas Clapp meant to find out, no matter the cost.

Nicholas Clapp was looking for a city, but he wasn't sure where to find it. No modern maps bore its name. No buildings marked the spot. No photographs showed how it looked. All Clapp had to guide him were stories. The city he sought was a lost one, perhaps even one that had never existed at all. Its name was Ubar.

Chapter 4 ~ **BURIED TREASURE**

Clapp, a Los Angeles filmmaker, first became interested in the phantom city in 1981, when he came across a few lines about it in a book by British explorer Bertram Thomas. Thomas, who had travelled into the Arabian desert in the late 1920s, described an ancient road he had seen on his journey. The road was choked with sand and broken in spots. It disappeared for long stretches, then reappeared again in other places. The road, Thomas said, led to Ubar. According to legend, Ubar had been a majestic city that stood tall and proud in the Arabian desert, attracting travellers from far and wide. Most historians, however, doubted that the city ever really existed. No trace of its tools, weapons or riches had ever been discovered. No one had found its walls or buildings. They believed the stories were just wild tales, told and retold so often that they almost sounded believable.

But Bertram Thomas claimed to have seen the road, and this fascinated Clapp. Maybe Ubar *was* real, he thought. Maybe it still existed somewhere beneath the Arabian desert.

Clapp dug into old history books, read reams of ancient documents, consulted experts on early cultures and searched for stories about the lost city. Books and papers filled his home, spilling from one room to another. Soon Clapp became lost in the subject, even forgetting to eat and sleep, but slowly he began to unravel the legend that was Ubar.

~

Thousands of years ago, a prosperous and powerful city stood on the southern edge of the Arabian desert. At its centre was a mighty walled fortress, guarded by tall towers at each corner and along the sides. Inside the fortress, surrounded by riches and comfort, lived a king, his family, servants and important officials. This was Ubar, city of riches, city of treasure.

Hundreds of makeshift tents dotted the hillside around the

fortress. Merchants and travellers lived there, all drawn to Ubar for the same reason — to barter and sell. Ubar was at the crossroads of several important caravan routes, and everyone, it seemed, came to the city with dreams of making a fortune.

The city's greatest treasure was hidden from view, below the ground in huge natural caverns the size of cathedrals. Water!

In the desert, water was a priceless resource, and Ubar had plenty of water beneath its sand. Ubar became a beacon for thirsty travellers and, from her deep reservoirs, palm trees, orchards and crops flourished in the hot sun.

For three thousand years, Ubar prospered. According to legend, wickedness and corruption slowly overcame the great city; then without warning, Ubar disappeared.

Some versions of the tale claimed that earthquakes caused the city to crumble and fall. Others mentioned a meteorite blazing to Earth, smashing the city to bits. Still other stories claimed that God had dealt the city its final blow, causing it to disappear into the sands as punishment for its evil ways.

Whatever the reasons, the stories agreed on one thing: Ubar had been erased without a trace, swallowed by the desert in an instant.

Inspired by his research, Clapp became convinced that Ubar had once been real, and he meant to find it. But how? If the city ever existed, it was now lost under the desert.

In his book, Bertram Thomas mentioned a road, and that seemed to be the most promising clue. Perhaps traces of the road still existed. Clapp just had to figure out how to find it.

By chance Clapp read a newspaper article that described how NASA used radar aboard its spacecraft to detect Mayan ruins. He wondered if NASA's radar could "see" buried roads, too. Clapp called Ron Blom, a geologist with NASA and one of

Chapter 4 ~ BURIED TREASURE

the authors of the article. Would NASA be interested in a search for the lost city? Clapp asked.

NASA was fascinated by the idea. The next year, during a space shuttle flight, NASA scientists scanned the Arabian peninsula, taking radar images of the desert. Clapp waited, nervous with anticipation. When Blom phoned with the results, Clapp held his breath, wanting to hear good news but prepared to be disappointed, too.

"There's definitely a road out there," Blom told him.

It turned out that there were many roads. Computer-enhanced images showed a spiderweb of lines, a crisscrossing network of roads, some modern, others ancient. One road, though, stood out from the rest. It was wider than most and matched the location described by Thomas. Cutting across the country of Oman, it ran from the coastal mountains in the south across a region known as the Empty Quarter, the largest sand mass on Earth.

Convinced he was on to something, Clapp spent years raising funds and locating experts for an expedition to Oman. By August 1990 he was ready. Guided by satellite maps, the crew flew over the desert in a helicopter, following the route identified earlier. They looked for traces of the ancient road. On satellite images it had appeared sharp, clear and well-defined. Closer up, though, the view was muddled, a confusing jumble of outcroppings, dunes and winding trails. The road could be anywhere.

Then, one day, as if by magic, they spotted it — a beaten path, wide and rutted, running across the desert, just as Bertram Thomas and the satellite images had promised. Was this the road to Ubar?

The road was broken and haphazard, visible for short distances, then gone again as it tunnelled under mountains of sand. Ubar, if it existed at all, could be anywhere, perhaps even along one of the many buried sections.

Now and then the team landed for a closer look. They checked ruins, gathered artifacts and questioned local tribespeople. Have you seen Ubar? they asked. No one had, but everyone knew its story.

> **The ruins turned out to be from a five-hundred-year-old fort.**

Once, when supplies ran low, the helicopter made an unscheduled stop at Shisur, a tiny oasis outside the search area. As they had done before, the team asked the villagers about Ubar. "Maybe not far away," one man told them. "Things get misplaced in the desert. But if the visitors are interested in ruins, there are, in fact, some here. They are just behind the tent."

The ruins turned out to be from a five-hundred-year-old fort. It wasn't old enough to be Ubar, and other than a few pieces of broken pottery, there was little of interest there. The crew left in a hurry, disappointed once again.

All in all, the expedition was a letdown. The desert was bleak, the heat unbearable. Sites that looked promising proved worthless. Clapp had invested almost ten years in the hunt for Ubar, but he had little to show for it. They had found traces of the road, but nothing of the city itself. Still, Clapp refused to give up. He made plans for a second expedition the following year.

In the meantime, once home, team archaeologist Juris Zarin sifted through the pottery he had collected on the expedition. Some pieces taken from different places bore similar dot-like patterns, he noticed. They seemed to have been made around the same time, by the same people, but came from widely separated places. Some even came from Shisur, which was far outside the search area. How could that be? Zarin wondered. How could the pottery have travelled to a place beyond the road itself?

Chapter 4 ~ **BURIED TREASURE**

Ron Blom was busy, too. He re-examined the radar images, tracing on them the route the expedition had taken. Had he missed something? As he flipped through the photos, Blom found an image he hadn't seen before. It showed a different section of the desert, the lines on it smaller and fainter than those on the other images. At least six lines crisscrossed one another. They intersected at a single spot in the Empty Quarter — the village of Shisur.

Blom noticed something else on the images, too. There were deep depressions in the ground at Shisur. Could this be an old sinkhole? Perhaps a collapsed underground cavern? Led by these new clues, the team returned to Shisur for a closer look in December 1991. The old fort, they found, had a central tower that had been oddly built. The base was square, carefully constructed, and appeared older than the rest. The top was round and seemed to have been built quickly and carelessly. The whole thing looked like a sloppily built sandcastle, with a round top resting on a much older square bottom.

Zarin started an excavation of the site. Every shovelful of rubble was screened, each object tagged and identified. During the second week of digging, the team unearthed a curved limestone wall and by following it, came to a strange horseshoe-shaped tower. More digging revealed other walls, more towers, all linked, all part of a massive octagonal fortress with a huge courtyard in the centre. In the courtyard the team discovered a well leading to an underground cavern.

There, pottery from ancient Greece was discovered, mixed with artifacts from Syria, Rome and other distant places. Some of the pieces were five hundred years old, others five thousand. While many of the objects were common household items, others were true treasures from the past — oil lamps, decorated chalices, carefully carved sculptures.

Was this Ubar? The evidence matched the clues provided by

Ruins of three-metre-wide walls and corner towers were found beneath the sands.

Clapp's research: a fortress city along a well-travelled caravan route, a hub of activity going back many centuries, a bustling centre of trade and commerce, a place with an unlimited source of water. But if it was Ubar, what had happened to the great city? The legend told of Ubar's violent end, of the city's disappearance into the sand. What could cause such disaster?

Ubar's greatest treasure may have also been its downfall. After centuries of use, the reservoir of water may have become drained, leaving the city standing on hollow ground. With such a weakened foundation, its collapse could have been triggered by an earthquake, leaving only memories of the once-great city.

From the memories, the tale of Ubar grew. Over the centuries, as the demolished city became covered with sand, that's all that remained — a story. One that led Nicholas Clapp on an extraordinary quest.

Treasure Tips

If there is something buried below ground, the best clues may be above . . . on the surface!

Bits and pieces
Erosion, land movements and human construction have a way of stirring up the soil, bringing evidence to the surface. Bits of bone, fragments of stone, coins or artifacts found on top of the ground could indicate that something important lies underneath.

Dip and mounds
Unexpected changes in the landscape can be signs of something below. Hollows or depressions in the ground could mean that the soil has settled over a structure or pit. Mounds or hills like the ones at Newfoundland's L'Anse aux Meadows could indicate that walls, buildings or garbage dumps are hidden underneath.

Plants and greenery
Plants in one area might be thicker, taller or greener than plants in another area. Such changes in growth could be due to hidden structures underground. For example, plants growing above a buried wall will be shorter than similar neighbouring plants because they are growing in shallower soil.

Other
Lost & Found Legends

Lost: Atlantis

Imagine a lush island paradise, rich in minerals, jewels and precious metals. Picture a city at its centre where people live in splendour around an immense palace covered in gold and silver. This is Atlantis, a legendary land described in writings left by Plato, a Greek philosopher who lived around 350 B.C. According to Plato, Atlantis met a terrible end. In a single day, the great civilization was swept beneath the sea.

Is there any truth to the story? Recently, archaeologists discovered evidence that thousands of years ago a volcanic eruption occurred on the Mediterranean island of Thera. The explosion created a huge cavity on the island, spewed volcanic debris into the atmosphere, and stirred the sea into gigantic waves. The eruption may have caused the destruction of the palace of Knossos on the nearby island of Crete, bringing the Minoan civilization that flourished there to a sudden end, and starting the legend that eventually became Atlantis.

Pushkin Museum, Moscow, Russia

Found: Treasure of Troy

In 1832 seven-year-old Heinrich Schliemann read Homer's *Iliad*, the legendary Greek story about an ancient walled city called Troy and its captive queen, Helen. While most scholars of the day dismissed the story as pure fantasy, the tale captured Schliemann's imagination. He searched the *Iliad* for clues to the city's whereabouts.

In 1870 Schliemann began to excavate a hill called Hissarlik in Turkey, a spot that matched descriptions in the *Iliad*. He unearthed a stone wall, then found an immense treasure of gold, silver and priceless jewels. To the amazement of everyone, Schliemann succeeded in finding not only Troy, but a legendary treasure as well.

 Machu Picchu, Peru

Found: Machu Picchu

Many years ago, a powerful people built a secret city in the mountains filled with beautiful palaces and glittering treasure . . . So began the South American legend that fascinated Hiram Bingham, an American university professor. In 1911 he led an expedition into the mountains of Peru to find the lost city. After weeks of fruitless effort, Bingham encountered a local who told him of ancient ruins at the end of a winding jungle trail up the side of a mountain. The ruins turned out to be a jumble of paved streets, private homes and temples perched high in the Andes Mountains. Although no gold or silver was discovered, Bingham had stumbled upon Machu Picchu, a forgotten city of the Inca. Today, the city has been restored and can be visited by hardy travellers bent on adventure and dazzling heights.

Lost: **The Lost Dutchman Mine**

A legendary "lost" mine lies somewhere in the Superstition Mountains near Phoenix, Arizona. In 1864 Enrico Peralta, a Mexican farmer, supposedly discovered gold there. According to the story, before Peralta could strike a claim, he was killed by a band of Apache who considered the mountains sacred land. A map sketched by Peralta fell into the hands of Jacob Waltz, a man nicknamed The Dutchman. Waltz supposedly found the mine hidden deep within a canyon. He kept its location a secret, visiting the mine only when he ran short of money and taking only as much gold as he needed on each occasion. When Waltz died in 1891, his secret died with him.

No proof has been found that the mine actually exists, but that hasn't stopped treasure hunters from searching. In the past century, dozens of people have tried to find the Lost Dutchman Mine. Many have met tragic ends. Some ran out of food and water or died of exposure after becoming lost in the mountains. Some simply disappeared. Others were found murdered, their corpses discovered with bullet holes in their skulls. According to one count, forty-four people have lost their lives trying to find the phantom treasure.

The British Museum, London, England

Beneath Mildenhall's Soil

The treasure remained hidden for centuries, 30 centimetres under the ground, until centuries later, when a farmer's plow forced it to the surface again.

On a January afternoon in 1942, a sharp wind swept through Mildenhall, England. Snow was in the forecast, and thirty-eight-year-old Gordon Butcher, a hardworking and reliable farmer, rushed to finish plowing a field before the blizzard struck.

The field was not Butcher's, nor was the job of plowing it normally his. A local man named Sydney Ford usually worked the field, which was owned by a man named Rolfe. But, as luck would have it, Ford was too busy to do the work and hired Butcher to plow Rolfe's field instead.

Around three o'clock, as the first few flakes of snow swirled to the ground, the plow snagged on something in the dirt. Butcher climbed off the tractor to take a closer look. He wasn't surprised, really — the soil often hid stones, roots and stumps of long-gone trees, and that's what he expected had happened. The plow had struck an object like one of these, bringing it to a standstill in the black soil.

Butcher knelt beside the plow, slid his hand into the dirt and felt around the blade. His fingers encountered an obstacle, something flat and round. A rock? A branch, perhaps? Butcher scooped away the soil and caught a glimpse of the curved rim of a disc. It was crusted with dirt, but when Butcher rubbed the rim, it glowed an eerie blue-green.

This was no stone, no battered stump. The object was made

of metal, corroded blue-green from years in the ground.

Butcher got to his feet. Objects like these were often found in fields in England. Centuries ago, the Romans had occupied Britain, and periodically people in the area unearthed their ancient pottery and tools. Perhaps that's what this was.

Unsure what to do, Butcher turned around and walked to Ford's place, not far away. Ford would know what to do. After all, Ford was a knowledgeable man, far wiser in the ways of the world than he.

Ford took an immediate interest, and accompanied Butcher back to the field. He shoved his hand into the dirt, feeling the round, flat object for himself. With a shovel, the two men dug deeper, carving a hole about a metre wide around the plow, revealing a huge round metal plate. More digging brought up other objects — dishes, bowls, goblets, spoons and ladles.

The weather took a turn for the worse, and snow began to fall. A blizzard was upon them, but the two men barely noticed, so intent were they on the objects in the ground. For an hour they dug, shovelling dirt aside, clawing with stiff fingers at the earth, eagerly tearing away chunks of soil. They unearthed thirty-four separate pieces, all metal, all crusted with the same blue-green material.

Satisfied at last that they had found everything, the men loaded the objects into a sack. Then they parted company, Ford hauling the sack to his place down the road, Butcher trudging empty-handed through the mounting snow to his brick house farther away. To Butcher, the find was interesting, but not one of great value to him. Chilled to the bone and anxious to get home, he was content to leave the sack with Ford.

Unlike Butcher, Ford knew that there was silver underneath the crust, and that the blue-green could be rubbed away with a little polish. He also knew that the objects were ancient — likely Roman — and that he had stumbled upon a prize of great

The Great Dish from the Mildenhall Treasure, also called the Oceanus Dish.
It measures 60.5 centimetres across and weighs more than 8 kilograms.

value. He decided to keep the hoard hidden.

Ford hid the objects in a cupboard, and each night, for months on end, brought them out one at a time to clean. Using silver polish and vigorous rubbing, he worked on the treasure, removing the blue-green deposits and letting the silver underneath shine.

But treasure laws in England were quite clear, and Ford knew what he *should* do — report the treasure. Gold and silver objects like these belonged to the Crown. They were national treasures, part of Britain's heritage, and not the property of a single person. In return for reporting the discovery, the finder would be rewarded, receiving not the treasure itself but the treasure's full market value. In this case, that would be a great amount of money.

Ford never reported the find. Butcher, who really found the treasure first, didn't either, so for years the fortune stayed secret, hidden in Ford's house, taken out only to be polished and admired, then hidden again.

All except for two silver spoons, that is. Two small spoons. Ford admired these greatly, and displayed them proudly on the mantle above his fireplace. This way he could enjoy their beauty any time he pleased.

The spoons were noticed by somebody else, and this became Ford's undoing. One day in April 1946 Ford had a visitor. Dr. Hugh Fawcett, a local archaeologist, stopped by as he did now and then. Ford was a collector of arrowheads and stone tools, and Fawcett hoped that perhaps he had something new and interesting to sell. Ford said nothing of the treasure, but as Fawcett turned to leave, he spotted two small objects on the mantle, two gleaming spoons bearing delicate carvings and curious inscriptions. Immediately, he recognized their Roman origins and their true value. Where did you find these? he wanted to know. Are there others?

Reluctantly, Ford showed Fawcett the other objects, then went to the police station to report the find. The treasure was collected and hauled to the British Museum, where it is on display today.

At an official inquest, the government claimed the treasure. Butcher and Ford were declared to be co-finders and, had they immediately reported the discovery, would have received the treasure's full value — estimated at up to a million British pounds. However, because they didn't report it, they were granted only a paltry £1000 each.

The Mildenhall Treasure, as the collection came to be called, dates to 400 A.D. and was likely buried by a wealthy Roman family to hide it from invading armies. No doubt the owner intended to return to dig it up when it was safe, but never did. It is the single most valuable find of Roman silver ever located in Britain.

The treasure remained hidden, 30 centimetres under the ground, until centuries later, when a farmer's plow forced it to the surface again.

Treasure Tips

Metal detectors help treasure hunters to "see" underground without even picking up a shovel. A metal detector tracks shifts in magnetic fields caused by objects in its path. When a metal detector sweeps over an object, it sends a sound signal to the operator. Besides pinpointing the spot where a buried object lies, the pitch, tone and volume of the signal can also tell the operator approximately how deep it is buried, what size it is, and the type of material it might be.

The Lost Squadron Museum, Middlesboro, Kentucky

The Lost Squadron

A dozen obstacles stood in their way, but the lure of the Lost Squadron was irresistible. The three men dreamed of finding the missing planes and flying one of them again.

July 1942

Wind whipped the P-38 fighter jet, pitching it wildly, threatening to push the plane off course. Clouds, thick and dense, hung like curtains on the horizon. Inside the cockpit the temperature plunged.

Lieutenant Joseph Bradley McManus, an American pilot, glanced at the fuel gauge. The needle flickered around empty. Could things get any worse? He was flying blind in a storm, on whispers of fuel, far from anywhere. He had to bring the plane down. Now.

McManus wasn't alone. There were seven other planes in his squadron — five more P-38s and two giant B-17 bombers. All eight planes — a total of twenty-five men aboard — flying together, all of them in trouble.

It was wartime. Allied forces were gathering in Britain, hoping to stop Hitler and the growing German threat. The U.S. squadron, all newly built planes, was on its way to lend a hand. Flying in a protective pack from the United States to Britain, the planes had stopped in Greenland to refuel and were heading to Iceland — one step closer to Britain, their final destination — when the storm struck. It was impossible to see, too dangerous to land, and so the planes were forced to turn back.

That's when they became lost. On the return to Greenland,

the cloud cover grew thicker, the wind wilder. The planes veered off course, gobbling up precious fuel the longer they flew. The tanks were almost drained by the time the pilots noticed that they were lost. The Greenland airfield was too far away to reach in time. They had to land the planes somewhere, anywhere, quickly.

McManus, the lead pilot, steered his P-38 below the clouds, skimming Greenland's snowbound surface, looking for a smooth spot wide enough to land. He decided one hard-packed patch would do. Lowering the wheels, he levelled the aircraft and aimed for the ground.

The moment the plane touched down, snow grabbed its wheels, twisting the plane, throwing it off balance. It flipped and skidded about 90 metres before slamming to a stop upside down. Slightly injured but safe, McManus waved to the others to come down.

> While waiting for rescue, the men of the Lost Squadron fired their .45s into the plane's electronic equipment and instruments. That way, if the enemy found the aircraft, the planes would be useless to them.

The second pilot attempted a landing with the wheels up. Snow flying, steel underbelly screeching, the plane skidded to a noisy stop. The other planes followed, dropping to the ice one by one, wheels up, each landing safely. All twenty-five men were grateful to be alive.

Someone radioed for help, and while they waited for rescue, the men transformed the B-17s into home base, sleeping inside one plane and using a helmet filled with gas and oil as a cookstove.

Rescuers arrived ten days later, two on skis, another riding a dogsled. They led the downed aviators on a 17-hour trek across wet snow and treacherous ice to two small boats. The boats carried them to a U.S. Coast Guard cutter which finally took them home.

The airplanes were left behind. There was talk of recovering them, of flying them again, but with war raging, that never happened. In the end, snow claimed the squadron. The planes became buried under a mountain of ice, entombed in an ever-growing glacier. Hidden from view, their exact location unknown, the squadron became lost.

Lost, but not quite forgotten.

~

Three Americans — Pat Epps, Richard Taylor and Roy Shoffner — knew of the Lost Squadron and shared a single dream: to find the missing planes and set one free.

Pat Epps was the first to get the dream going. Being a pilot himself, he had taken a special interest in the stories he'd heard of the Lost Squadron. He became obsessed with finding the planes and convinced his friend, architect Richard Taylor, that it might be worth a try.

Over the years there had been many attempts to locate the planes. All of them had ended in failure. The planes were well hidden, buried under mountains of shifting ice, perhaps crushed or mangled. Even if they could be found, would there be anything left to salvage? No one knew for certain.

In 1981 Epps and Taylor flew to Greenland and skimmed over the spot where the squadron had last been seen. Since the tail of a B-17 is taller than most houses, the men expected that at least a piece of it would still be jutting through the snow. To their surprise, they found nothing. The planes were buried deeper than they thought.

The two men rented a pair of high-powered metal detectors and set up a grid system over the ice. They walked across it, taking readings and plotting any shifts they detected. The results were wildly different each time. The metal detectors were unreliable, and the men finally flew home, disappointed

Chapter 4 ~ BURIED TREASURE

and no closer to their goal than before.

In 1986 Epps and Taylor returned, this time with better equipment and a crew of assistants. Again, they found nothing. In 1988 they tried once more, expanding the search, dragging radar on a snow sled over a grid several football fields in size. Just as Epps and Taylor were about to call it quits and head home, they detected a faint signal near the outskirts of their search area.

To investigate what lay below, the crew shot steam into the ice, melting holes around the region of the signal. At a depth of 76 metres the probe hit something, but before they could explore further, the weather soured, forcing them to leave. There was something far below the ice, but the men would have to wait to find out what it was.

In 1989 they returned with a core drill, a device that draws samples from below and brings them up for inspection. Again at 76 metres they hit something metallic, and when they pulled up the drill and checked the bit, there it was — a piece of aluminum. The Lost Squadron couldn't be far away.

But how could they reach the planes? The ice was rock hard and the planes were too deep to reach with ordinary equipment. To solve the problem, in 1990 the crew dragged in a new contraption, a huge torpedo-shaped device called the Super Gopher. The Super Gopher was suspended by chains over the ice, its tip just above the surface. Solar-heated water was fed into the nose of the Super Gopher to slowly melt the ice below, creating a shaft more than a metre wide. Pumps suctioned off the meltwater, keeping the hole clear.

The Super Gopher worked slowly, melting ice at a snail's pace — barely a metre every two hours. Storms buried the equipment under new snow, and temperatures dropped so low that the crew had to stop working for days at a time. Finally, after weeks of tunnelling through the ice, the Super Gopher came to a halt, its nose bumping up against an obstacle.

The Super Gopher had come to rest on the bent propeller of a B-17. The plane had been found, but the aircraft was a shambles, flattened and mangled under tonnes of ice, and beyond repair. Discouraged and too broke to continue, Epps and Taylor packed up and went home yet again.

In 1992 they returned with renewed hope and another partner — Roy Shoffner, a Kentucky businessman. The B-17 had been a mess, but had all the planes met the same fate? P-38s were smaller, more durable than B-17s. Perhaps one of them had survived the crushing ice. The crew aimed the Super Gopher at a different spot and started melting another shaft in the ice. This time they struck pay dirt — a P-38.

> **Would the years of effort and hundreds of thousands of dollars invested be worth the price?**

Epps was one of the first to be lowered into the shaft to check the new-found plane. He dangled from a cable attached to a harness, his body clad in a bright orange rain suit, a miner's hat atop his head. Behind him came Shoffner, who described the half-hour experience as being "like sliding down a soda straw." Excitement was tinged with dread. What would they find? A mangled mess like the B-17? Or would the years of effort and hundreds of thousands of dollars invested be worth the price?

Hot water had been sprayed around the fighter plane, creating a huge cavern far below the surface. Once Epps and Shoffner reached the bottom, they stepped into a scene straight out of 1942. In front of them was a piece of history — a P-38 from the Lost Squadron. Its body was dented, its bolts and rivets loosened, its paint scratched by half a century of moving ice, but the plane was still intact and looking much like it did long ago. The crew dubbed the fighter plane Glacier Girl.

P-38 Glacier Girl is hoisted out from its icy burial place.

Finding the plane was only the first step. Next came the most daunting phase — melting the ice around the plane, taking it apart, raising it to the surface one piece at a time and sending the parts by helicopter, ship and truck to Kentucky for reassembly and restoration.

The recovery and refurbishing of Glacier Girl took patience, skill and money. Restoration crews worked on the fighter jet out of an airport hangar in Middlesboro, Kentucky, keeping parts that were salvageable and making new ones to replace the old when that was not possible. More than 80 percent of Glacier Girl's parts came from the original aircraft. Others were custom built to original specifications. Eventually Glacier Girl was moved to a permanent home, a specially constructed facility known as the Lost Squadron Museum.

On October 26, 2002, ten years after being raised to the surface, Glacier Girl was flown again. As the plane soared into the

Kentucky sky, her aluminum shell smooth and shiny as new, a little of the 1942 air saved from the original tires pumped back into her new ones, Epps, Taylor and Shoffner watched from the ground. For the men it was a crowning moment, a dream fulfilled. The Lost Squadron had been found. A piece of history had been recovered and set free.

~

Every World War II P-38 pilot who visits the museum is asked to inscribe his name, rank and serial number on a bullet from the plane. On her maiden flight in 2002, these bullets were carried aloft in Glacier Girl for "extra good luck."

Other Lost & Found Wartime Treasure

The British Museum, London, England

Hidden Hoard

Eric Lawes went looking for a hammer. He found Roman treasure instead.

In 1992 Eric Lawes used a metal detector to search for a friend's lost hammer in a farmer's field near Hoxne, Suffolk, England. After receiving a clear signal, he stooped to clear away the soil from the spot. A few centimetres below the surface, he found a silver coin the size of his thumbnail. Lawes dug deeper, and unearthed other gold and silver wonders — bracelets, chains, pendants and hundreds of coins. Realizing there was still more treasure in the hole he had created, Lawes placed the items he'd found in the trunk of his car, then reported the find to authorities.

Archaeologists found more coins and other objects, as well as metal hinges to a long-decomposed wooden box that might have held them. In all, 14,780 coins were recovered as well as assorted jewellery, pepper pots, ladles, silver toothpicks and silver spoons. Historians believe that the treasure had been hidden in the ground sixteen hundred years ago by a wealthy Roman family during a time of war. For some reason, they never returned to claim it.

Today, the Hoxne Hoard can be seen in the British Museum in London. For his part in the discovery, Eric Lawes received its estimated value — £1.75 million.

 The Catherine Palace Tzarskoje Museum,
Pushkin, Russia

Lost: The Amber Room

It would seem difficult to lose a room, but one has vanished without a trace. It's worth from $100 to $300 million, to boot!

The Amber Room was originally built in 1701 in the Charlottenburg Palace near Berlin by Friedrich I, King of Prussia, who had a fondness for the finer things in life. It took his artists ten years to cut, carve, polish and assemble over a hundred thousand pieces of amber, a rare crystal-like substance that comes from trees. They produced a stunning room covered in the glimmering material.

In 1716 the room was dismantled and brought to St. Petersburg, Russia, by Czar Peter the Great. Later, it was carted to the nearby suburb of Tzarskoje Selo (now called Pushkin) by Peter's daughter, Empress Elizabeth. There it stayed for almost two hundred years.

On June 22, 1941, during World War II, Germany invaded the country. Workmen packaged paintings, bundled sculptures, and hauled palace treasures into the surrounding mountains for safekeeping. The walls of the Amber Room were too delicate to be moved. The palace staff hurriedly wallpapered over them, hoping to fool the approaching Germans.

The plan failed. Two German officers recognized the

Amber Room. Quickly it was dismantled and shipped by train to Koenigsberg, a German-controlled city, where it was installed on the third floor of the Koenigsberg Palace.

By April 1945, the tide of war turned once again, and German officials worked feverishly to hide their stolen treasures. Six men, working thirty-six hours, dismantled the room and packaged it into twenty-seven crates. And that's where the trail of the Amber Room runs cold. The room simply disappeared and hasn't been seen since.

A replica of it now exists, however. Working from pre-war photographs, thirty artisans spent twenty-four years meticulously rebuilding the room, replacing each of the missing pieces with new ones all carved from amber. The new Amber Room can be seen in The Catherine Palace Tzarskoje Museum, Russia.

Lost: European Art Treasures

As Adolf Hitler steamrollered across Europe during World War II, he ordered the plunder of banks, museums, archives, synagogues, churches and private art collections. Paintings, silverware, sculptures, jewels, books and furniture were catalogued, photographed, crated and hauled to secret locations around Europe. One of the caches was in a salt mine at Alt Aussee in Austria. There, in a maze of rooms, corridors and tunnels deep underground, over twenty-seven thousand pieces of stolen art, jewellery and church relics were stored.

At the end of the war, Allied forces discovered the Alt Aussee site as well as other locations of hidden Nazi loot. Many of the stolen items were returned to their rightful owners, but other objects have never been found. It is estimated that one fifth of the Nazi hoards are still concealed in secret locations throughout Europe.

Found: Synagogue Treasure

In 1998 Yariv Nornberg, a young soldier, stopped to buy a flag in a convenience store in his hometown of Ramat Hasharon, Israel. The ninety-year-old owner, Yishayahu Yarot, said he was out of stock, but asked Nornberg to return the following week. When Nornberg explained that he could not because he was supposed to fly to Poland to tour concentration camps from World War II, the old man told him, "I was born in Poland. I was born in Auschwitz . . ." Yarot went on to describe a secret he had been keeping for almost sixty years.

In 1939, with the Nazis occupying the town of Auschwitz, Yarot had seen three men from the synagogue there place a number of precious religious objects in two metal boxes. To hide them from the Nazis, the boxes had been buried in the ground. During the war, the synagogue was destroyed and its location and that of the boxes were lost and forgotten.

Nornberg's request for a flag triggered Yarot's memory of the event, and the old man was able to draw a map pinpointing the location of the boxes. Led by the map, Polish archaeologists found the remains of the destroyed synagogue. Beneath it, they unearthed a wealth of artifacts, including four golden menorahs, a lamp and several chandeliers.

 Hungarian National Parliament, Budapest, Hungary

Found: Crown of St. Stephen

The history of the Crown of St. Stephen reads like a spy novel. According to legend, the crown was given to St. Stephen, the first king of Hungary, by Pope Sylvester II in 1000 A.D. Since then the jewel-encrusted golden crown has been hidden, lost, captured, stolen and rediscovered a number of times. Its most recent disappearing act occurred during World War II.

In May 1945, as they travelled through Germany, a group of Hungarians was stopped and searched by American soldiers. They carried a suspicious-looking iron-bound chest. When the large chest was opened, it was found to be empty. What had been inside? the soldiers asked. The Crown of St. Stephen and other royal jewels, the travelers eventually admitted. They confessed to removing the objects from the chest for safekeeping, hiding them in an oil barrel, then sinking it in a marsh near the village of Mattsee. The marsh was searched, the barrel located, and the crown jewels removed. They were sent to a bank in Frankfurt. Then they vanished.

For twenty years the location of the precious crown with its 53 sapphires, 50 rubies, 1 emerald and 838 pearls, remained a mystery. Then, in 1965, the United States admitted that the crown was in American hands. It had been squirreled away all these years, the government said, kept under tight security, waiting for a time when it could be safely returned to its rightful owners — a free nation of Hungarian people.

In January 1978 the Crown of St. Stephen and the rest of the royal jewels were handed over to officials in Budapest, Hungary — ending the adventures of the well-travelled crown.

Chapter 5
SURFACE TREASURE

In Their Own Words

"I didn't exactly hear voices, but something kept pulling me there. Something wanted it to be me that went there and found her."
Sue Hendrickson, explaining the eerie circumstances that led to her outstanding fossil find

"It made a clanging noise when it hit another rock . . . I was thinking right away, oh wow, this was silver or gold or something else."
Derek Erstelle, describing the unusual rock he picked up while moose hunting

"Oh god, I have found it!"
Johannes Makani, upon discovering the Jonker diamond

"Look, Daddy, bulls!"
Five-year-old Maria de Sautuola's excited reaction to her discovery in Altamira Cave

The Field Museum, Chicago, Illinois

Sue Finds Sue

From far away, Sue Hendrickson heard the call. Something — or someone — wanted her to come to the remote sandstone cliff.

It was hot the morning of August 12, 1990. Foggy, too, which was very unusual for the Badlands of South Dakota. Normally in August the sun rose like a fireball over the parched landscape. That day, it was shrouded behind a veil of mist.

Fog hovered over Maurice Williams's ranch, too. It wrapped itself around hills that rose from the rocky field, like humps on a camel's back. An 18-metre sandstone cliff in a remote corner of the ranch was hidden by the fog, but Sue Hendrickson knew it was there. It had been calling her for some time.

Hendrickson, a self-taught fossil hunter, was on the last day of a month-long dig. While the rest of her crew headed to town, Hendrickson stayed behind and listened to the call. Something, someone important, was beckoning her to the cliff. "I didn't exactly hear voices," she explained later, "but something kept pulling me there. Something wanted it to be me that went there and found her."

Hendrickson loaded a few belongings into a backpack and drove to the edge of Williams's ranch, her dog, Gypsy, with her. After parking the Jeep, she began the 11-kilometre hike to the cliff. In the heavy fog, it was hard to get her bearings, and after two hours, Hendrickson ended back at her starting point — she had walked in a complete circle. But the call was still strong and the pull to the cliff unmistakable. Hendrickson waited patiently for the fog to lift, then she started again, walking another two hours before finally arriving at the base of the cliff.

Its steep sides were coated with fragile layers of pebbly rock. Rubble covered the ground at the base, and, as was her habit, Hendrickson started her search there. She looked for bone fragments, chips and pieces that might have broken off larger bones embedded in the cliff.

Halfway through her walk-around, Hendrickson noticed a bunch of bone scraps on the ground. She looked up just above eye level, and poking through the rock she spotted a number of bones. To get a better look, she carefully scaled the cliffside.

Four bones protruded from the rock — a string of three vertebrae and one femur, a leg bone. Instantly Hendrickson knew she was on to something amazing. These were dinosaur bones. Ordinarily that would be thrilling enough, but there was something even more special about these particular dinosaur bones.

For one thing they were unusually large, which meant the dinosaur must have been immense, too. Plant eaters had flat vertebrae, but these were slightly curved, the telltale sign that the dinosaur had likely been a carnivore. When Hendrickson picked up bone scraps at the base of the cliff, she noticed another oddity. The bones felt light for their size, as if hollow.

Only one dinosaur matched the clues. Really big . . . carnivorous . . . hollow-boned . . .

Tyrannosaurus rex.

Because the bones jutted from the rock, Hendrickson felt there might be many more bones hidden behind. A whole skeleton, perhaps? She could only hope.

Until that time only eleven *T. Rex* had ever been found. This would be the twelfth and, judging from the size and condition of the bones, perhaps the largest and most complete.

"I didn't jump up and down and scream. But I was thinking, Wow! What was so cool was that the vertebrae were mostly going into the hill, so it looked like the potential for more."

Chapter 5 ~ SURFACE TREASURE

Hendrickson scooped up a handful of bone fragments from the base, then raced back to camp. Eagerly she showed them to Peter Larson, her boss and head of the Black Hills Institute of Geological Research. He was immediately interested.

Hendrickson guided Larson to the site, running most of the way across the open field. The signs were all there, he confirmed. This was a *T. Rex*, a massive one, and very possibly a complete one at that.

> **They still hadn't found the skull ... the most important bone.**

"Call it intuition or whatever, I just knew," Larson explained later. "I knew this was gonna be the best thing we'd ever found and probably ever would find."

Larson rallied his crew, and within two days they were there ready to dig — shovels and picks, cameras and sketching pads at the ready. Already they had formed a personal attachment to the creature, affectionately calling it Sue after its discoverer.

The team started by gathering all the scraps from the ground and putting them in carefully labelled plastic bags. Then, to protect the protruding bones, they applied a hardener and covered the bones with burlap and plaster of Paris. Next they chipped away the cliff, removing the overhanging rock and exposing the bones. Each bone was mapped and charted before being removed. In some cases entire chunks of surrounding rock were crated and carted to the lab for further processing.

For more than two weeks, the crew patiently unearthed Sue, freeing it from the rock that had contained it for millions of years. They were growing anxious, though. They still hadn't found the skull. In many ways it was the most important bone, the piece that would complete the dig and provide more information about the animal than all the other bones. It was also the piece that most often went missing. Because the skull is attached to the skeleton with only a few vertebrae, it is usually the first thing to drop off during decomposition. Separated from the rest of the body, skulls often disappear, washed away by many millions of years of rain and mud, leaving the remains headless and incomplete. The crew hoped that wasn't the case with Sue.

On the sixteenth day of the dig, they finally located it. "It was the last bone," Hendrickson recalled. "We had literally the whole skeleton . . . We had almost given up on it, and we were digging around the pelvis, which was huge — as big if not bigger than the skull — and we dug a wide mushroom around it to get it out of the ground. And the skull was underneath."

Like the rest of the skeleton, the skull was massive. Weighing 272 kilograms, it was 1.5 metres long. Its razor-sharp teeth were enormous, with the longest tooth a record-setting 30 centimetres. Back in the lab, the bones were chiselled from the rock, cleaned and repaired. Then, for five years, they languished in a heavily guarded building while courts decided who owned their rights. In the end they were auctioned off for

The *T. Rex* skeleton dubbed Sue, on display at Chicago's Field Museum.

US$8.36 million to the Field Museum of Chicago. The money went to Maurice Williams, the rancher who owned the property where Sue was found.

How did Sue Hendrickson profit from the treasure she unearthed? While she did not share in the fortune the skeleton commanded at auction, she is all right with that — money has never been the issue. For Hendrickson there are more important things: the hunt for new fossils and the unravelling of mysteries from the past are what keep her going.

She does have a strong attachment to Sue, the *T. Rex*, however. Occasionally she drops by the Field Museum to look at Sue. "Emotionally, I'm very, very tied to her," she says. " . . . I don't want to sound weird, but there's a very strong emotional tie. And yes, I feel very much her mother, her finder, whatever."

Treasure Tips

Fossils are remains of prehistoric animals and plants that have been preserved in rock. Often fossils are found deep below the surface, in areas of sedimentary rock where the ground has been layered in deposits from ancient seas or oceans. Alert treasure hunters can sometimes find fossils on the surface, however, when wind, water and man-made conditions expose them and bring them to the top. Streams, rivers, coastlines and windswept regions are likely spots for finding surface fossils, as are roads, fields and areas where the ground has been mixed and turned.

Meteorite Graveyard

As soon as Derek Erstelle picked up the stone, he knew it was different. Was it made of gold, silver or something even more precious?

The day when Derek Erstelle's fortune changed is as fresh in his mind as yesterday. When he tells his story, it's like he's still there, picking his way through the forest, hunting moose, not expecting that day to be any different from a dozen other similar days in his life. But that day was anything but ordinary.

That morning in September 2002, Erstelle was hunting moose near Bernic Lake in Manitoba's Whiteshell Provincial Forest. Being an experienced hunter, Erstelle knew the region well. The forest was thick with trees, so dense and heavy that "you couldn't see up, you couldn't see down, you couldn't see side to side." The air was misty with drizzling rain, the ground slick and slippery. The forest was perfect cover for moose, and Erstelle knew they were there, camouflaged by their surroundings. With patience and skill, he would find them.

By noon Erstelle was hungry and cold. He stopped in a clearing to make a fire. After digging a shallow pit in the damp soil, he looked for stones to circle the pit. Spotting some that were jutting out of the underbrush, Erstelle picked up a few at a time, lugged them back to the pit and tossed them on the ground.

That's when his luck shifted.

As soon as he picked up one stone in a nearby ravine, Erstelle knew it was different. "It looked like every other rock there. The only difference to it was its weight and the sound it made when I dropped it. It made a clanging noise when it hit another rock, so it told me right then and there that it was metallic. I was thinking right away, oh wow, this was silver or gold or something else."

Chapter 5 ~ SURFACE TREASURE

Then Erstelle found a second stone about 4 metres away. Like the first, it was unusually heavy for its size and felt metallic.

All his life Erstelle had been a rockhound. Collecting minerals, gems and rocks was as natural to him as hunting moose. Although he didn't know exactly what the two stones were, he knew they were different, and that was enough to pique his curiosity. He hauled the stones out of the forest and brought them home.

For a whole year, Erstelle forgot about the stones. He used one as a doorstop for his patio door. He stored the other in a box in his garage. Then, at the suggestion of a friend, he cut a small fragment from one of the pieces and sent it to be analyzed by the Prairie Meteorite Search, a Canadian research project that encourages prairie farmers to have rocks they find checked to see if they might be meteorites.

The fragment fascinated researchers at the Prairie Meteorite Search. They identified it as a meteorite — a piece of an asteroid from outer space. When Erstelle explained that the fragment came from one of two stones found in the same region, their interest grew even more. Together, the pieces weighed 9.8 kilograms, making them sizable and important chunks of space debris.

Meteorites — fragments of asteroids that once orbited between Mars and Jupiter — are evidence of another time and place far beyond the boundaries that Earth imposes. Millions of years ago, an asteroid must have wandered astray and

> *Finding one fragment from an asteroid was rare enough. Finding a second one was extraordinary.*

entered the Earth's atmosphere, exploding in a fiery display before plunging to the ground near Bernic Lake.

Finding one fragment from an asteroid was rare enough. Finding a second fragment from the same asteroid was extraordinary.

Rockhound Derek Erstelle displays one of the meteorite fragments he found.

Erstelle's discovery got him thinking about the other rocks in his collection. Many had come from the same region as the meteorite. Did he have other meteorites like this among the rocks he kept at home? Erstelle dug into dusty boxes, sifting through dozens of rocks, looking for any that seemed heavier than normal or appeared metallic in nature. He hauled out a 2.5-kilogram rock that seemed to fit the bill. He'd found it in 1998 near Pinawa, a town about 40 kilometres from Bernic Lake.

Chapter 5 ~ SURFACE TREASURE

In July 2005 the Prairie Meteorite Search team identified it as having come from a second meteorite. Tests showed that it had come from a different asteroid, making this discovery even more remarkable than the first. Had Erstelle stumbled upon some kind of meteorite graveyard? Were there other meteorites awaiting discovery in the south-eastern region of the province?

That summer, Erstelle headed back to the Whiteshell area equipped with binoculars and metal-detecting equipment. Like a hunter stalking prey, he crept through the forest, watchful of stones and outcroppings that seemed different from others. When he spotted red-colored gravel through his binoculars, he knew he was on the trail of something big. The pieces turned out to be rusting, iron-rich chunks from yet another meteorite.

Iron-rich meteorites may be rusted from long exposure and appear red in colour. Because of their high iron content, magnets may be attracted to them.

As a discoverer of fragments from three different meteorites, Erstelle's name belongs in the record books. No other Canadian has found two meteorites, let alone three. But his discoveries are extraordinary in another way, too. Because all of the meteorites were found in the same region, scientists suspect that Erstelle has stumbled upon something truly rare — a dump site for meteorites.

Over eleven thousand years ago, glaciers covered much of North America. Meteorites that crashed to the region during this period became trapped in the ice. As the glaciers melted, they retreated and drew northward, carrying the meteorites along with them and eventually depositing them at the edge of the dwindling ice sheet.

Scientists such as Dr. Alan Hildebrand, one of Canada's top meteorite experts, believe that the Bernic Lake region is especially rich in meteorites because two lobes or arms of ice met there, one coming south from Hudson Bay and the other coming north from the Prairies. Much as objects are carried on a conveyor belt, meteorites on the twin lobes were likely transported to the edges, producing a dump site of sorts for space debris.

"I think hundreds of thousands of meteorites are entirely possible," Dr. Hildebrand says.

While important for the scientific information they provide, meteorites are valuable in another way. When his first meteorite was sold to the Royal Ontario Museum, Erstelle received a cut of its $50,000 price tag. But it's not just money or fame he's after.

"Meteorites are the poor man's space program," he told a reporter. "You can spend much of your life without thinking too much about space, so whenever there's a meteorite find, you get a chance to explore the solar system a little bit."

For Derek Erstelle, finding meteorites is a lifelong passion. "Treasure is everywhere if you know what to look for," he maintains. And Erstelle knows that other treasures — perhaps vast numbers of them — may lie deep in the forest around Bernic Lake.

Treasure Tips

• When meteorites fall to earth, they plow into the soil, creating impressions in the ground. Small meteorites leave pockmarks, some no larger than the head of a pin. Larger meteorites make crater-like depressions. Although depressions are best seen from the air, they can also be spotted by alert treasure seekers on foot.

• Meteorites, especially ones with metallic cores, often feel heavier than other rocks their size, and make a clanging metallic sound when struck. They may have a burnt crust and depressions that look like fingerprints on the surface.

• Although meteorites fall everywhere on earth, the chances of finding one are best in desert areas or prairie regions. The ground there is flat, largely free of vegetation, and constantly exposed to weathering elements that bring buried objects back to the surface.

More Lucky Strikes

Money from Heaven

In 1992, while a woman sat watching television in her home in Peekskill, New York, a 12-kilogram meteorite smashed into the trunk of her car. The accident turned out to be a profitable one. The woman sold the meteorite to a collector for US$68,000. The car, dented and damaged by the freak accident, became a collector's item, too. It was valued at $300 at the time, but sold for more than $10,000.

Dirty Glass?

On January 17, 1934, Johannes Makani was washing a bucketful of gravel near a mine at Elandsfontein, South Africa, when he spotted something unusual in the rubble. The rock was caked with dirt, but it was distinctly different in shape and colour from the others.

After scrubbing the object, Makani immediately recognized it for the treasure it was. Throwing his hat in the air, he shouted, "Oh god, I have found it!" It took Makani awhile to convince Johannes Jonker, his employer, that the chunk of dirty-looking "glass" was actually an ice-white diamond the size of an egg. At the time of its discovery, the Jonker Diamond was the world's fourth largest at 726 carats.

Since then the diamond has changed hands several times. In 1977 it sold in Hong Kong for an estimated £1.25 million.

Golden Nugget Casino, Las Vegas, Nevada

Million-Dollar Hand

The world's largest gold nugget can be seen at the Golden Nugget Hotel and Casino in Las Vegas, Nevada. Called the Hand of Faith because the 28-kilogram nugget is in the shape of a hand, it was found in Victoria, Australia, in 1980. Kevin Hillier discovered it just 15 centimetres beneath the ground behind his mobile home. The casino purchased it for US$1 million as a tourist attraction.

The Louvre, Paris, France

Venus de Milo Revealed

Two men — one a simple farmer, the other a French naval officer — found the statue. Now they were locked in a battle for possession. Who would own it and what was its real worth?

Every day visitors come to the Louvre, the largest museum in Paris, to gaze at a statue of a woman. Its arms are missing. It is scratched and chipped. Yet it is one of the world's great treasures.

The statue is famous, but few know the story of how, had it not been for two men, the statue might never have made it to the Louvre.

~

Yorgos, a farmer living on the island of Melos in the Mediterranean, tugged on the stones along the crumbling old wall of an ancient Greek theatre. It was April 8, 1820. Some of the stones were loose and just the right size for the structure he was building at his home a short distance away. Others were too large or irregularly shaped to be of much use. Yorgos tossed these aside.

> *The statue was beautiful, perhaps, but useless.*

In the ruins, Yorgos spotted a promising piece smothered with dirt. He dug around it, tearing it loose, dragging it into the open to examine it carefully. The piece was larger than he first thought. Oddly shaped, too, and smoothly polished.

A statue. Beautiful, perhaps, but useless to the farmer.

~

Twenty paces away, twenty-three-year-old Olivier Voutier toiled in the dirt. The French naval officer's ship was stationed in the harbour, leaving him with little to do. The day was a fine one, though, to indulge in one of his passions — archaeology. Voutier had heard that there were ruins on the island of Melos and that on this very spot there had once been an ancient Greek theatre. There was a market for antiquities, Voutier knew. Museums all across Europe were eager to acquire new statues and artifacts for their collections. Perhaps with a bit of digging he'd find something special.

Voutier convinced two sailors to accompany him. Armed with picks and shovels, they chipped at the ruins, dismantling

Chapter 5 ~ SURFACE TREASURE

walls and foundations, tearing apart the ruins one stone at a time. In short order they had unearthed a number of valuable items — a carved foot and two broken statues, among others.

From the corner of his eye, Voutier spotted another man. A local farmer, it appeared. Like them the man had been digging, but now he had stopped and was standing motionless, staring at something he had unearthed. Curious, Voutier wandered over.

Yorgos stared at the carved block for some time. It was a delicate piece — but it was of no value to him. It was too large, heavy and lopsided. He was best to leave it.

Yorgos shovelled dirt over the stone, then stopped when Voutier came near. Voutier stooped low, momentarily entranced. What was this, a marble statue? A piece of one, at least, lying on its side, partially buried.

"Dig some more," Voutier implored. He offered Yorgos money to continue. The farmer readily agreed, dreams of new-found wealth taking hold. Slowly, with more digging, a statue rose from the dirt. It was the nude upper half of a woman. The statue's torso was chipped and scraped, its nose broken and arms missing, the carved surface stained from centuries in the dirt.

Even though it was damaged, Voutier sensed there was something extraordinary about the statue. Its features were delicate and graceful, the lines simple but elegant. Clearly the statue was ancient and the work of a skilled artisan.

But where was the rest of the statue? There had to be more. A base, at the very least. Voutier offered the farmer more money. Yorgos dug, flinging dirt and rubble aside with even greater zeal. A second piece emerged, and then, with a bit more searching, a third one, smaller than the other two.

The three pieces fit together like a puzzle, and the two men set about reconstructing the statue. They piled up the pieces — a base at the bottom, the delicately carved torso on top and the third smaller piece in between, acting as a sort of wedge keeping the whole thing balanced. They stepped back to take a look. The statue was larger than life-size, majestic and breathtaking.

The statue rightly belonged to Yorgos. After all, he had been the first to find it. But Yorgos clearly didn't want the statue. He wanted money instead, and Voutier knew that for the right price the statue could be bought. He scurried away to find a government official on the island. The statue must be claimed for France, he decided, and only a representative of the French government could do that. "Watch the statue," he told Yorgos. "I'll be back."

> **One of the marble pieces found near the statue identifies the sculptor who created the Venus de Milo. The inscription on it translates to "Alexandros, son of Menides, citizen of Antioch of Meander."**

While Voutier was away, Yorgos dug some more. He found a marble hand holding an apple, a badly mutilated piece of an arm, and two pillars, each with a carved head on top. By the time Voutier arrived with the government official, Yorgos had reevaluated the treasure. He wanted more for the statue now. Enough, at least, to buy a good donkey.

The French official, Louis Brest, hesitated. Should he dish out the money from his own pocket? What proof did he have that this statue was a masterpiece? All he had was the word of Voutier, an amateur archaeologist.

Brest refused to close the deal. "Not today," he explained. "I'll be back in a few days if I'm interested." Then he left. Discouraged by Brest's decision, Voutier gave up. He headed back to his ship, determined to forget the whole thing.

But Yorgos didn't forget. Nor was he discouraged. The statue was worth money, he figured. Even if the French were not interested, others might be. Yorgos lugged the upper half of the

Visitors who go to see Venus de Milo at the Louvre will find another famous piece of art there, Leonardo da Vinci's famed Mona Lisa. The two are among the most recognizable art treasures in the western world.

statue to a cowshed near his home along with the arm fragments, broken hand and two pillars. He left the base and middle piece behind. They were not worth as much, he reasoned, and were not as likely to be stolen.

The top half of the statue sat in the cowshed for days, surrounded by manure and straw and guarded by Yorgos's mother, who sat at the door. Eventually Brest returned with other French officers. After much dickering they submitted to Yorgos's demands, giving him the money he requested. The complete statue — all three sections and the other pieces found nearby — was carefully crated and shipped to France.

The statue arrived in Paris in February 1821 and was presented to Emperor Louis XVIII, who immediately named the statue Venus de Milo. In Greek mythology, Aphrodite (Venus) is the goddess of love. The figure, scholars believe, once adorned a temple. When the temple was destroyed, devoted worshippers must have hidden the statue in a chamber to protect it.

> *The Venus de Milo draws amazing crowds wherever it goes.*

Today the Venus de Milo stands in an alcove of the Louvre, its three main pieces reassembled, the seams between them almost invisible. Resurrected from the dirt by two men with very different motives, it is one of the world's greatest treasures.

~

The Venus de Milo draws amazing crowds wherever it goes. When France loaned the statue to Japan in 1964, more than a hundred thousand people came to greet the ship carrying it, and one and a half million people viewed the statue itself when it was put on display.

Other Puzzling Treasures

 National Archaeological Museum of Athens,

Athens, Greece

The Right Fit

In 1928 a bronze figure of a boy jockey was found in the wreckage of a sunken ship off the coast of Greece. In 1937 other bronze fragments were found at the same site. It took archaeologists a while to realize that the fragments were sections of a larger figure — a horse. It took them even longer to realize that the boy jockey belonged on the horse. Today, the Horse and Jockey of Artemision can be seen in the National Archaeological Museum of Athens, reunited at last after twenty-three hundred years of underwater separation.

Recycled Wonder

More than two thousand years ago, a giant bronze statue of the Greek sun gold Helios towered 37 metres above the harbour at Rhodes, a small island in the Mediterranean Sea. Standing on a huge marble pedestal, one hand clutching a sword, the other holding a torch, the warrior-like figure guided ships into the harbour.

Because of its size and weight, the Colossus, as the statue was called, was not built of solid metal; instead, it had a hollow core. It was made of individual bronze sheets that were bolted together and supported by iron struts inside it. In 224 B.C. an earthquake rocked the island. The Colossus toppled, snapping into house-sized pieces. For hundreds of years the broken statue lay where it had fallen, attracting visitors who came to stand and stare at this once-great wonder of the ancient world. Then in 653 A.D. the metal supports were dismantled. Bit by bit the Colossus was sold for scrap and shipped to neighbouring countries around the Mediterranean.

Although the statue has long since disappeared, in a curious way it may still survive. The scrap metal was melted and recast into new tools, weapons and ornaments. It is possible that some of these objects may exist even today.

But the statue at Rhodes survives in another way, too. In 1886 a modern colossus, built in the same fashion as the ancient one, with metal sheathing supported by iron struts, was erected in New York's harbour — the Statue of Liberty.

National Archaeological Museum, Naples, Italy

Closer Look

Sometimes it takes a person with a keen eye to spot a real treasure standing right in our midst. Such was the case with the Farnese Atlas, a marble statue 2 metres tall that stands in the National Archaeological Museum in Naples, Italy. The statue shows a muscular man, crouching under immense strain, holding a huge globe on his shoulders. The man is the Roman god, Atlas, and the globe shows the position of forty-one constellations in the night sky.

Chapter 5 ~ **SURFACE TREASURE**

The Farnese Atlas was carved in the second century A.D., and that by itself makes it treasure enough. But there's something else about it that boosts its value even more, something not discovered until 2004 when Bradley Schaefer, an American astronomer, took a closer look.

Curious about the constellations, Schaefer took measurements of their positions on the statue's globe. Knowing that the locations of stars in the night sky change over centuries, Schaefer compared the positions of stars in the present-day sky to those on the globe. By noting the changes he was able to assign a date to the view of the sky shown on the Farnese globe.

Schaefer came to a startling conclusion. The Farnese globe showed constellations from around 125 B.C., almost three centuries before the statue itself was made. Schaefer believes that the sculptor who made the Farnese globe must have based the star positions on a much earlier work — a star catalogue made by the Greek astronomer Hipparchus, who lived around that time.

Although Hipparchus's original catalogue has long vanished — possibly lost in a fire in the great library of Alexandria, Egypt, where it may have been stored — Schaefer may have rediscovered a treasured copy of the ancient astronomer's work right where it's been for centuries: on the shoulders of an ancient statue right under our noses.

The British Museum, London, England

Key to the Past

In 1799 French soldiers demolishing an old fort near the town of Rosetta, Egypt, unearthed a strange black stone. It was flat, irregularly shaped, the size of a table top. Carved into the stone were three sets of markings, each in a different language, each appearing to repeat the same message. One was in hieroglyphics, the picture writing that adorned pyramids and temples of ancient Egypt.

At the time, no one knew how to interpret hieroglyphics. The language had been lost and forgotten in the passage of time. The other two languages on the stone were known to scholars, however, and this raised their hopes. Would it be possible to crack the hieroglyphic code by matching the symbols in the message to the two other languages on the stone that possibly said the same thing?

Many language experts tried to solve the ancient puzzle. All failed. Then, starting around 1809, Jean-Francois Champollion, a young Frenchman, gave it a try. A master of ancient languages, Champollion recognized that hieroglyphic symbols stood for *sounds*, rather than words. This was the key to unravelling the ancient language. Decoding the symbols on the Rosetta Stone consumed Champollion for the rest of his life. In the end, he gave us not just a method of interpreting a lost language, but also the keys to understanding an ancient civilization.

Chapter 5 ~ **SURFACE TREASURE**

The Shrine of the Book: The Israel Museum,
Jerusalem, Israel

Brittle Bundles of the Dead Sea

The cave was dimly lit, but as Muhammad's eyes grew accustomed to the darkness, he saw in the shadows tall jars — rows of them — standing on the rocky floor. One of them was broken.

That day in 1947 started out as it usually did for Muhammad Adh-Dhib, a young Bedouin goatherder. The sun blazed in the sky, as it almost always did, making the desert between Bethlehem and the Dead Sea scorching hot. As was his habit, young Muhammad let the animals in his care roam about the rocky hills in search of food while he rested.

But one of the goats wandered too far, and that, as it turned out, made the day remarkable — even extraordinary. Muhammad followed the animal, climbing high among the rocks until, hot and tired, he stopped to catch his breath in the cool shade of an overhanging cliff. As he rested, Muhammad spotted a small hole in the cliff face, about a half metre wide.

Idly Muhammad picked up a stone, took aim and tossed it into the opening. He stooped to pick up another stone, then stopped. What was that sound? He had expected to hear the clatter of the stone striking the rocks in the cave or perhaps the thud of the stone hitting its sandy bottom. Instead he heard a crash, as if something had been broken. Muhammad threw another stone. Again he heard the smash of something breaking.

Curious now, he scampered up the rough cliff face, grabbed hold of the jagged rocks around the hole and pulled himself up. The cave was dimly lit, but as his eyes became accustomed to the darkness, he spotted tall jars, rows of them, standing on the rocky floor. One of the jars was broken.

Suddenly Muhammad became afraid. No human could live in such a small cave, he thought. Desert spirits must live here. And now he had disturbed their dwelling. Wasting no time, he dropped to the ground and ran off as fast as he could.

The next day, his courage restored, Muhammad returned with a friend. The two squeezed through the narrow opening and dropped themselves inside. Rows of jars lined the narrow cave, some with lids, others without. Several jars were empty, but one contained bundles of rags so brittle that they crumbled at a touch. Inside one bundle the boys could see a black tarry substance and below that, smooth brown leather.

Later, when the boys untied and unrolled the bundles, they discovered they were scrolls covered with strange markings. Unable to understand the writing, the boys rewrapped the scrolls and took the bundles to Bethlehem. At a general store, they traded the scrolls for food. Curious about the markings, the merchant took the scrolls to Jerusalem, where he showed them to a monk at a monastery. Did he know what the scrolls said? The scholarly monk studied them carefully, recognizing passages from the Bible. Slowly he turned to question the storekeeper. Where did he find the scrolls? Were there any more to be had? Could he lead others to the spot? Immediately the storekeeper realized that the crumpled scrolls had more value than he had first thought.

The storekeeper located the cave and removed more scrolls while the monk organized his own expedition to the site and retrieved others. Word of the find spread like wildfire across the desert. Others visited the cave, taking anything they thought could be sold. The small cave opening was enlarged. Items that seemed to have no value, such as the broken jars and linen wrappings around the scrolls, were tossed in a heap outside.

Prof. Bieberkraut unrolling the Genesis Apocryphon.

Eventually, archaeologists heard of the discovery. Teams of scientists travelled to the area to search through the surrounding hills. Eleven caves were discovered, and in them the remains of over eight hundred separate texts dating to the period from 250 B.C. to 100 A.D.

Every effort was made to track down and obtain the scrolls that had been taken by the treasure seekers. This was no easy task — often the scrolls had been broken up in order to increase their value. They were in thousands of pieces, in dozens of different hands.

After years of hunting and haggling, many of the fragments were gathered, but a massive undertaking still remained. Like a gigantic jigsaw puzzle, the pieces had to be reassembled. The dry desert air had prevented rotting, but now the pieces were too brittle to handle without further breaking. The fragments were dusted, treated in a humidifier to return some moisture, then laid between sheets of glass on long tables. Because the edges were torn, an exact fit was impossible.

In time many of the fragments were matched and assembled. The Hebrew and Aramaic writing was translated and samples of the linen wrappings dated. What a treasure had been found! It wasn't gold or jewels. But the Dead Sea Scrolls, as the writings came to be called, proved to be rare texts, many of them written centuries before the time of Christ.

To scholars this was a priceless prize. Some of the scrolls contained Biblical passages. Before the discovery of the Dead Sea Scrolls, the earliest written records of the Bible had been

Greek and Latin translations dating from the fourth century. Now, for the first time, it was possible to study the Bible in a much more authentic form.

There were non-Biblical documents among the scrolls that were important, too. They described a little-known period of history and a group of people known as the Essenes, who likely wrote the Dead Sea Scrolls and lived in the area where the caves were found.

In the more than fifty years since their discovery, dozens of scholars have studied the Dead Sea Scrolls. Even today the work continues. Not everyone agrees on their meaning or the interpretations given them, and debate about the origins and importance of the scrolls is ongoing. Few would argue, though, that the Dead Sea Scrolls are one of the most significant discoveries of all time. They are, in the eyes of many, treasure in its truest sense — a cache of priceless documents discovered by a curious Bedouin boy in search of nothing more than a wayward goat.

Fragments of what has been called The Isaiah Scroll, found in Qumrun.

Other
Kid-Found Treasures

Steps in Time

In August 2000, nine-year-old Daniel Helm and eleven-year-old Mark Turner were tubing down Flatbed Creek near Tumbler Ridge, British Columbia, when Mark fell into the water. The boys waded ashore. On a long, flat slab of rock alongside the creek, they spotted four indentations in the surface. To the boys, the pattern of impressions in the rock looked like footprints — giant, fossilized footprints! Dinosaur tracks, they figured. Rich McCrea, a dinosaur trackway expert, agreed. When he investigated the site, he discovered twenty-two other prints nearby, as well as a number of dinosaur bones. From the size and spacing of the footprints, McCrea pieced together a story of the past. Ninety-five million years ago, an ankylosaur about 6 metres long, 2 metres tall and moving around 2 kilometres per hour tramped through the region, leaving modern-day humans with a lasting impression of its prehistoric journey.

 Lascaux Cave, Lascaux, France

Hidden Passage

In September 1940 three boys playing in the woods in south-western France fell into more adventure than they imagined possible. Some say the boys were looking for a secret passageway. Others say they were led to their discovery when a dog accompanying them ran ahead and became stuck in a hole. Whatever the version, what remains true is that the boys stumbled upon a remarkable find — the entrance to a tunnel in a ridge known as the Lascaux hill.

Seventeen-year-old Marcel Ravidat, the oldest boy, was the first to squeeze through the hole. Far inside the narrow passageway, he found himself in a large cavern. The walls and ceiling were decorated with colourful paintings of horses, bison, antelope and other animals. Tests showed that the paintings were fifteen to twenty thousand years old. Because the cave had been protected from heat, sunlight and weather for so long, the colours were as vibrant as the day the pre-historic painters put them on the walls.

 Altamira Cave, Santidel Mar,
Cantabria, northern Spain

"Look, Daddy!"

Curiosity won the day in 1879 when Don Marcelino de Sautuola and his five-year-old daughter, Maria, searched a newly discovered cave in northern Spain. Sautuola, an amateur archaeologist, was interested in finding artifacts, so he kept his eyes on the floor. Maria, on the other hand, was interested in far more, gazing up and all around. When she wandered into one of the cave's side chambers, the light of her lantern played on the ceiling. "Look, Daddy, bulls!" she cried as she ran to her father. The ceiling of Altamira Cave, they discovered, was filled with brightly coloured paintings of animals. The paintings, the handiwork of prehistoric artists, had been hidden and preserved in the cave for fourteen thousand years.

Devil's Coulee Dinosaur Heritage Museum,
Warner, Alberta

Shell Fragments

On May 24, 1987, Wendy Sloboda of Warner, Alberta, was exploring the Milk River Ridge when she stumbled upon some unusual fossil fragments. Suspecting they might be dinosaur egg shells, the teenager carefully collected the bits and sent them to Dr. Len Hills of the University of Calgary for identification.

Wendy's instincts were correct. Dr. Hills sent the fragments to Dr. Philip Currie of the Royal Tyrrell Museum in Drumheller, Alberta. Currie confirmed that the fragments were dinosaur egg shells. That summer a survey crew was dispatched to search the area. Near Devil's Coulee, one of the crew, Kevin Aulenback, noticed a small bone sticking out of the ground at the bottom of a hill. Knowing that fossil debris tends to roll downhill, Aulenback looked up. On the side of the hill, he saw bits of eggshell and part of an egg with a tail sticking out of it. The Devil's Coulee site proved to be a hadrosaur (duckbill dinosaur) nesting site, the first ever found in Canada.

In 1997 Sloboda made another significant find in the same region. She uncovered a nest of ten football-sized dinosaur eggs, the largest collection ever found in Canada.

Natural History Museum, London, England

Awesome Anning

Mary Anning grew up along the English coast, an area rich in sea fossils. In 1810, when Anning was only eleven, her father died and her family took to fossil hunting to earn extra money. Mary soon proved to have a keen eye for fossils. After a storm tore away part of a cliff, she spotted a bone protruding from the dirt. It turned out to be the first complete skeleton of an ichthyosaur ever discovered.

This wasn't Mary's only find. In 1823 she discovered the first-ever skeleton of a plesiosaur, and in 1828, fragments of a pterodactyl. Today, Mary Anning's ichthyosaur is on display in the Natural History Museum in London, England.

Epilogue

You, the Treasure Hunter

Treasure hunters come in many varieties and so do the treasures they seek. Each hunter of treasure has a different view of what is rare, valuable or important. To a prospector, treasure may be gold. To an archaeologist, it's an artifact that tells about the past. To a diver, treasure may be a shipwreck on the ocean floor, while to a stamp collector it is a new stamp added to the collection.

Treasure hunters differ in their reasons for seeking treasure, too. For some, the motive is fame or great fortune. For others it is personal satisfaction in knowing they have achieved a long-sought goal. Others are motivated by the knowledge that the treasure brings. For them, new understanding, not wealth, is the aim of the hunt.

Despite their many differences, most treasure hunters share a common bond, whether they seek pieces of eight, a long-lost tomb or a new comic book for a collection. For many treasure hunters, it's the hunt for the prize that provides the biggest thrill, more than the prize itself. The adventure, excitement and satisfaction of the quest are what drive most treasure hunters through hardships and disappointment, around dead ends and wrong turns, down twisted roads to their final destination — the treasure.

What is treasure for you? What are your reasons for seeking it? Diving for sunken chests of gold or travelling to remote islands may be out of the question right now, but there are other ways you can satisfy the treasure hunter inside you.

Begin Collecting

A great way to begin treasure hunting is with a collection. People collect all kind of things: stamps, coins, comic books, baseball cards, dolls, CDs, toys, arrowheads, minerals . . . Objects like these that are collected for pleasure or for profit are called collectibles.

Pick something you are interested in collecting and learning about. Start small and add to your collection when you can. Read all about your chosen treasure. Knowledge is power when it comes to collecting. Discovering what to look for, where to find it and what makes items in your collection valuable or important is part of the fun.

To learn more about the objects in your collection, you might try the Internet. Some sites provide background information about particular collectibles that could prove useful when you are starting out. Some list items for sale. By comparing the asking price and condition of these articles, you can get a rough idea of the value and significance of your own. (Collectibles that are in excellent condition and in high demand, but are also not very plentiful, usually fetch the highest prices.)

Join a Club

Many clubs, organizations and associations are rooted in treasure. Interested in stamps? Look for a philatelic (stamp-collecting) society in your community. Are fossils your passion? There may be a mineral and fossil group right around the corner. Perhaps metal detecting suits you better. Many cities have metal-collecting clubs whose members meet regularly and go on excursions to hunt for buried objects. For the names of treasure groups near you, browse the Internet or check the Yellow Pages under Associations, Organizations or Clubs.

Brake for Treasure

Many of the world's greatest treasures are on display at historical sites or in museums and galleries around the globe. Make a point of visiting these places if you're going to be travelling to the area.

Volunteer to Dig

Volunteers are often enlisted to help at dig sites. Working side by side with archaeologists and paleontologists looking for artifacts and fossils can provide valuable training in the ways of treasure seeking. Contact a museum, archaeological society or historical society in your region for information about ongoing digs and to see if there is some way that you can volunteer.

Hit the Racks

Check the magazine racks of a bookstore or your local library for magazines such as *Lost Treasure*, *Western & Eastern Treasures*, *Gold Prospectors*, *Rock & Gem* and *World Coin News*. Not only will you find treasure stories written by other readers, you can often get tips and helpful information on how to proceed. Many magazines have websites that can lead to other sources, too.

Game It

Geocaching is the latest treasure-seeking game. Someone hides "treasure" in various locations, and then posts the positions on the Internet. Using a hand-held global positioning system (GPS) receiver, treasure hunters follow the clues to find the hidden cache. Geocaching is for adults, but if you have a parent or other responsible adult willing to accompany you, you can play, too.

Treasure Hunting Laws

Not all treasure hunters' goals are alike. Imagine two divers searching for a lost shipwreck and the treasure in its hull. What if one is dreaming of striking it rich, of finding the treasure and selling it to the highest bidder? What if the other is an archaeologist, wanting it to be preserved and studied for the information it provides about the past? Because the goals are different, the divers will differ in how they proceed.

To protect treasures and settle treasure hunting differences, many countries have laws to govern how treasure should be handled. The laws, however, often vary from one country or province to another, and they depend a lot upon the kind of treasure being sought and the places it is located.

In general, you can treasure hunt on private property if the owner of the property agrees. Treasure hunting on public property or Crown (government-owned) land, such as beaches, parks or walkways is another matter. Some public places may be accessible to treasure hunters. Others are definitely not.

Historical or cultural sites are protected by law — even picking up an object there can get you into trouble. In 2005, for example, a Canadian girl was arrested for picking up a stone at Greece's Parthenon. Despite her claims that she only wanted to take a photo, authorities charged her with illegally possessing antiquities and jailed her briefly before releasing her.

If you find treasure, even on private property where you have permission to search, do you get to keep it? Sometimes. A lot depends on the type of item found, who owned it previously and how it came to be lost or misplaced.

With a little "digging," you can find out what rules apply to your situation and region. Check with museums, government agencies, metal-detecting clubs, professional dive shops and the Internet for the information you need.

The Treasure Hunter's Code

Although treasure hunting laws vary, there are some guidelines that all treasure hunters can follow. Many metal-detecting clubs and treasure seeking groups have a code of honour that guides their search. Here is a typical version of the Treasure Hunter's Code:

• Be courteous to fellow treasure hunters and others you meet. Share your knowledge and experience.

• Respect and obey all existing laws. Seek treasure only in areas where it is legally allowed and where you have obtained permission from the landowner or other authority. Use methods that preserve and protect the treasure and its surroundings.

• Avoid restricted public areas such as archaeological and historical sites. In most cases these are protected by law and are off limits to all treasure hunters except qualified archaeologists, scholars and historians with permits allowing them to explore these areas.

• If you find an artifact, fossil or site that might be important, do your best to leave it intact, and report your discovery to the authorities. Leave the hunt area in its original clean and tidy state.

• If you do find treasure, follow these rules:

Lost treasure If the owner of a lost item can be identified, you must return it. However, if the owner cannot be found, you may keep it as long as the landowner has given you permission.

Hidden treasure If you discover a treasure that has been purposely hidden by its owner, the treasure rightfully belongs to the original owner and his/her heirs, if they can be located.

Stolen treasure Stolen property belongs to the original owner. If, for example, you find a can stuffed with hundred-dollar bills buried in your yard and the serial numbers on the bills can be linked to the loot stolen during a bank robbery, the treasure belongs to the bank, not to you.

INDEX

INDEX

INDEX

Illustrations by David Sourwine

Photo credits

Also by Larry Verstraete

Mysteries of Time Vanished peoples, hidden documents, secret graves . . . Discover how to uncover the secrets of the past.

Whose Bright Idea Was It? True stories of invention, inspired by strange circumstances, even by accident! Finalist for the Silver Birch Award; nominated for the Red Cedar Award; a Canadian Toy Testing Council Great Book for Children; *Emergency Librarian*: Top Outstanding Books for 1997.

Accidental Discoveries: From Laughing Gas to Dynamite Fortunate fumbles, surprise endings — the goofs, coincidences and twists that resulted in amazing new discoveries. Shortlist, Norma Fleck Award, 1999; CBC Radio Recommended Reading List.

Extreme Science Many scientists risked their reputations, even their lives, to make new discoveries. Real stories of scientists who ventured into the danger zone. *ResourceLinks Magazine* — Best of the Year 2000.

Survivors! True Death-Defying Escapes True hair-raising stories of people who survived floods, lightning strikes, avalanches and more. PLUS key survival tips for dangerous situations. Winner of the Silver Birch Award; shortlisted for the Red Cedar Award.

For Further Reading

Bazrod, Sondra Farrell. *The Hunt for Amazing Treasures.* New York: Dell Publishing, 1999.

Clapp, Nicholas. *The Road to Ubar: Finding the Atlantis of the Sands.* Boston: Houghton Mifflin Co., 1999.

Claybourne, Anna, and Caroline Young. *The Usborne Book of Treasure Hunting.* London: Usborne Publishing Ltd., 1999.

Clifford, Barry. *Expedition Whydah.* New York: Cliff Street Books, 1999.

Deem, James M. *How to Hunt Buried Treasure.* Boston: Houghton Mifflin Co., 1992.

Fiffer, Steve. *Tyrannosaurus Sue.* New York: W. H. Freeman and Company, 2000.

Flaherty, Thomas H., ed. *Lost Treasure.* Alexandria, Virginia: Time-Life Books, 1991.

Hayes, David. *The Lost Squadron.* London: Bloomsbury, 1994.

Holdcroft, Tina. *Hidden Treasure: Amazing Stories of Discovery.* Toronto: Annick Press Ltd., 2003.

Kelsey, Elin. *Canadian Dinosaurs.* Toronto: Owl Books, 2003.

Lincoln, Margarette. *The Pirate's Handbook.* Toronto: Scholastic Canada Ltd., 1995.

Paine, Lincoln P. *Ships of the World: An Historical Encyclopedia.* New York: Houghton Mifflin Co., 1997.

Pickford, Nigel. *Lost Treasure Ships of the 20th Century.* Washington: National Geographic Society, 1999.

Reid, Struan. *The Children's Atlas of Lost Treasures.* Brookfield, CT: The Millbrook Press, 1997.

Ritchie, David. *Shipwrecks: An Encyclopedia of the World's Worst Disasters at Sea.* New York: Facts on File, 1996.

Wagner, Kip. *Pieces of Eight: Recovering the Riches of a Lost Spanish Treasure Fleet.* New York: E. P. Dutton & Co. Ltd., 1966.

Wilson, Derek. *The World Atlas of Treasure.* London: William Collins Sons & Co. Ltd., 1981.

Wright, John. *Lost Treasure.* New York: The Bookwright Press, 1989.